2049

SUPERNORMAL GROWTH

China's Economy 1979–2049

1979

Jeffrey Zhengfu SHI
Fudan University, China

2049

SUPERNORMAL GROWTH

China's Economy 1979–2049

1979

World Century

Published by

World Century Publishing Corporation
27 Warren Street, Suite 401-402, Hackensack, NJ 07601

Library of Congress Cataloging-in-Publication Data
Shi, Zhengfu, 1954–
[Chao chang zeng zhang. English]
Supernormal growth : China's economy 1979–2049 / by Jeffrey Shi Zhengfu (Fudan University, Shanghai, China).
pages cm
Translation of the author's Chao chang zeng zhang.
Includes bibliographical references and index.
ISBN 978-1-938134-62-3
1. China--Economic conditions--1976–2000. 2. China--Economic policy--1976–2000. 3. China--Economic conditions--2000– 4. Economic forecasting--China. 5. China--Economic policy--2000– I. Title.
HC427.92.S5365313 2015
330.951--dc23
2014035226

British Library Cataloguing-in-Publication Data
A catalogue record for this book is available from the British Library.

Originally published in Chinese

Published by arrangement with SCPG Publishing Corporation and Shanghai People's Publishing House.

In-house Editors: Dipasri Sardar/Philly Lim

Typeset by Stallion Press
Email: enquiries@stallionpress.com

Printed in Singapore

Dedicated to Zhai Li — my wife, my best friend and my partner.

The Tao begot one.
One begot two.
Two begot three.
And three begot the ten thousand things.
*Laozi, Tao Te Ching, Chapter 42**

The defect of the feudal system is that power exercised arbitrarily by local authorities, while the defect of the centralized imperial system is that all power concentrated at the top. If a sage king arises who can apply feudal principle to the imperial system he will then bring peace to all under Heaven.
Gu Yanwu, "The Complete Works of Gu Yanwu — The Collected Poems of Tinglin" Volume 1 "A Discourse on the Imperial System" **

---

* Laozi, "Tao Te Ching," Trans. Jane English, Feng Gia-fu, Vintage Books, 1989.
** Shanghai Guji Chubanshe, 2011.

Contents

Preface

In the past 30 years or more, the Chinese supernormal growth has created an unprecedented "China Miracle." Reflecting on this marvel of growth throughout the human history, was it just a flash in the pan? Or was this China's contribution of oriental wisdom to the history of human development? Looking to the future, can such a supernormal growth be sustained and, if so, how?

Wise men have said, "How we interpret the history will determine how we choose the future." Therefore, the key to answer the questions raised above lies in firstly finding out how this "China Miracle" came about.

Some said that it can be attributed to the curbing of consumption. In the past 34 years, consumer spending accounted for about 59% of China's gross domestic product, while investment was 38%. Compared with conventional market economies, this percentage of consumer spending was low and investment relatively high. However, the growth of China's consumption scale or consumption level has been astounding. During the same period, if we take 2011 as the base year for constant prices, total consumer spending rose from more than RMB1.3 trillion in 1979 to about RMB24 trillion by 2011 — the average annual growth rate reached 9.12%; in terms of per capita spending, average growth was about 8.05%, taking the top place among medium(or above)-sized economies.

Others argued that it is due to a reliance on excessive investment. As shown above, it is true that the investment rate in China was significantly higher than in developed Western countries as well as in other East Asian economies with comparatively high savings ratio. However, it might not be the case when perceived from the capital–output ratio, a more comprehensive indicator the reading stayed at 3.38 in the first decade of the reform and opening up and 4.10 in the last decade, these readings are not higher than some developed countries. For example, between 1965 and 2010, the capital–output ratio in the US was 5.29, and between 2005 and 2009, when affected by the financial crisis, it hit 22.64. In Japan, the rate was 14.69 between 1980 and 2010, soaring to 37.16 between 2000 and 2010. Historically speaking, although China's ratio climbed, it was not due to overinvestment, but rather a reflection of the objective economic laws behind the historical process of industrialization and mass-scale urbanization. As this process deepens and the tertiary industries expand, the capital–output ratio will stabilize or even decline slightly.

Another argument is that China's achievement is a result of its demographic dividend. Certainly, the sheer number of population in China ensured an effective supply of workforce and the demographic dividend contributed greatly to China's economic growth. However, when observing other Asian countries such as Japan, South Korea, Singapore, Malaysia, Indonesia, the Philippines and Vietnam which have also benefitted from the demographic dividend one after another, it is not difficult to notice that there are huge differences of economic development level among these economies. This means that a demographic dividend does not necessarily lead to economic growth.

So what is the underlying reason for China's supernormal economic expansion? The answer is: the socialist market economy with Chinese characteristics.

The socialist market economy with Chinese characteristics is a three-dimensional market structure that consists of strategic central government, competitive local governments and competitive enterprises. It is a ground-breaking economic system that dynamically combines the strategic leadership of the central government, local governments' impetus for development and the innovative vitality of enterprises. The formation and evolution of this institutional arrangement under China's socialist market economy marks that China has initially established a new type of economic system which is systematically different from those conventional Western-style market economies.

In this three-dimensional structure, the competitive enterprises, focusing on innovation and development, is the micro body for resource allocation; the competitive local governments construct a sustainable "investment incentive system," lowering the investment costs for new ventures and thus increasing the equilibrium level of investment. They also provide business services, similar to what corporate headquarters do, and assist enterprises to break through ministry bureaucracy, creating a super vigorous driving force for the investment in Chinese economy; the central government, based on its fundamental role to make long-term plan for national economic growth, considers all-around and ensures a balance between development and stability on the one hand. And on the other, by seizing the opportunity of globalization, it managed to assess the timing and decisively made the whole nation integrate into the world's division of labor system, effectively absorb the "supernormal international purchasing power" provided by US's deficits in consumption, fiscal budget and trade. This has created additional market opportunities to accommodate China's high investment, high growth rate economy.

It is the supernormal investment force and supernormal international purchasing power generated by such a socialist market economy that prevent China from the periodic economic crises which are inevitable in conventional market economies, and thus have created a miracle of co-existence of supernormal growth and super-low economic fluctuation during the two decades of high-speed growth since 1994.

Of course, the more than 30 years of China's development has been very complicated and multifaceted. Behind the brilliant accomplishments, there have been many problems that needed resolving, such as the absence of owners of the SOEs and monopolies, the overly large income gap and the unfair distribution of wealth, an excessively large government, disorder in the market, official corruption, environmental pollution, etc. These problems are either the phenomena associated with the development in China at current stage or endogenous outcomes resulting from the operation of the market economy. These deficiencies could only be solved via governmental reform instead of further marketization of the economy. If we said the theme of the first 30 years of reform began with a deconstruction of the planned economy and then creation of markets, then the second round would be the organizational transformation and administrative process reengineering.

As the reform moves on, the socialist market system with Chinese characteristics will continue to operate effectively as the institutional foundation of China's supernormal growth. However, the international purchasing power will eventually disappear as the global financial crisis spreads. From a long-term perspective, consumption upgrading, industrial upgrading, urbanization, informationalization and agricultural modernization herald a huge market demand and room for development in the future. But this demand is a normal function of the market economy and correspondingly, conventional economic growth. To realize supernormal growth, demand must come from some third-party beyond the market system. Previously, this was international purchasing power based on excessive issuance of US dollars. In the future, what kind of a similar long-term purchasing power could replace it?

The answer has actually been indicated in the question. On the one hand, it is inevitable for China to accumulate an large scale of savings under conventional market. On the other hand, there are a number of constrains on the supply side that will impact on future growth. From energy security and ecological construction to human capital accumulation and high-tech innovation, all require long-term and large amounts of capital investment. In relative to Western developed countries where the natural environments are well preserved, this investment should be regarded as the necessary "extra investment" in order to form the nation's basic assets. In relative to the objective of achieving the future well-being of the people and the long-term stability of the nation, this should be taken as the required fundamental work for the constructing of a harmonious society. Therefore, the key to the realization of supernormal growth in the future is to find a suitable mechanism which is capable of pairing the "excessive savings" with the "extra investment" so as to resolve the difficulties of both sides at the same time.

To this end, one option would be to establish a comprehensive national strategic development fund, which can be operated for long-term investment in ecological assets and strategic resources. In this process, a new type of supernormal purchasing power will be created and injected into the conventional market economy, and meanwhile, the national fundamental assets of strategically significance can be established and operated perpetually. This is the pivotal point of this book. We could say that investments in strategic bottleneck factors, such as ecological assets, land redevelopment, clean energy resources and human capital, which emerge as a sequel of the supernormal purchasing power, are not dispensable public projects. Instead, they are fundamental projects of strategic significance which are essential to the long-term development of the nation and the well-being of the people. And if they are carried out properly, they can offer desirable returns over the long-term.

We can fully expect that by the centenary of the founding of the People's Republic of China, the country will be among the leading nations in terms of GDP and per capita GDP. At the same time, the socialist market economy will demonstrate its great systemic competitive advantages in the institutional competition globally; as a development path differed from those classic Western ones, while serving as the most critical basis for the great rejuvenation of the Chinese nation, it also offers an alternative institutional option for human civilization and, therefore, contributes China's wisdom to the diversified evolution of human society and civilization. With confidence in this course, this theory and this system, China's road ahead will surely be stable and exceptional.

About the Author

Jeffrey Shi Zhengfu was admitted to Fudan University's department of economics in 1977, earning a bachelor's degree in economics in 1982, a master's in 1984 and then staying on to teach. In 1985, Shi traveled to the US to pursue his studies, earning a doctorate of economics at the American University and a doctoral candidacy at the University of Maryland's Department of Sociology. During his time in the US, Shi also worked as a *contract researcher at the US Department of Labor's Division of Economic and Labor Research.* After returning to China in 1995, Shi entered into business and founded Shanghai Comway Capital Group, where he has been serving as chairman since then. In 2003, Shi was invited to serve as the director of Fudan University's Center for New Political Economy. Shi also concurrently serves as director-general of *Jiao Tong University's Research Center for Global Finance in Shanghai* and adjunct professor at Nanjing University, and a member of the academic committees at Tsinghua University's Center for Political Economy and the Boyuan Foundation. Shi has authored the following books: "Structure and Management of Modern Enterprises"; "Labor and Value in Modern Enterprises — a Modern Expansion on Marx's Labor Theory of Value"; "The Revolution in Property Rights in Modern Enterprises"; "Rationality and Path Dependence in Agricultural Reform: The Origin of China's Pattern of Reform Governance." Shi has also co-authored "An

Analysis of Socialist Macroeconomics" and "A Textbook for Political Economics" among dozens of other Chinese and English-language academic papers. Shi has been a recipient of many academic honors including the Sun Zhifang Economic Science Prize Award and the China National Book Award.

Chapter 1

China's Unconventional Economic Growth

The supernormal growth of China's economy, which was brought about by the policies of reform and opening up, has continued for 34 years, becoming a marvel in the history of world economics. To call it a marvel is not only because of the rapid economic growth, but more importantly, because the path to growth has eclipsed the known models of industrialization in developed countries.

As we know, modern industrialization developed almost two hundred years and was first completed in the United Kingdom. It was then followed by Continental Europe, the United States, Canada, Australia and New Zealand. In Asia, it was Japan and the so-called Four Asian Tigers that experienced a similar pattern of development, their fundamental institution consists of market economy based on private enterprise, party politics based on competition, society of law based on legislation game and procedural justice, and national interest based on global competition. This system of development for national economies is widely accepted as the orthodox or "normal" model for modernization.

However, from the start of reform and opening up, China has worked out a development path different from the mainstream model described above. From the pace of growth, economic cycles and the government's structural functions to income distribution and the social distribution of wealth and other important areas, it can be seen that China's experience exhibited new and different traits compared with those early developed countries. If we took the models of development of those early developed ones and called their economic growth "normal," then China's growth from the start of the reform and opening could be described as "supernormal."

Professor Justin Yifu Lin initially discovered and expounded upon the theory of China's supernormal economic growth. He also refined and gradually developed the theory of New Structural Economics.[1] Lin proposed that a country's optimal industrial structure is determined by the comparative advantages of its factor endowments. Therefore, upgrading the industrial structure in a given country requires a transition of its factor comparative advantages; and the discovery and growth of comparative advantages and the optimal industrial structure must be based on competition among firms in the market. Meanwhile, the government is highly needed to play an active role in aspects such as infrastructure construction, selection of advantageous industries as well as promoting and guiding industrial upgrade. Professor Lin's theory of New Structural Economics explained how many developing nations rashly pursued failed catch-up strategies and also demonstrated the likelihood of success if a government implemented development policies in a market economy. Therefore, New Structural Economics helps us to understand how China's development

[1]Justin Yifu Lin, Cai Fang and Li Zhou, "Zhongguo Qiji: Fazhan Zhanlue yu Jingji Gaige (Zengdingban) [The China Miracle: Development Strategy and Economic Reform (Revised Edition)]," Truth and Wisdom Press, SJPC and Shanghai People's Press, 2012; Justin Yifu Lin, "Xinjiegou Jingjixue: Fansi Jingjifazhan yu Zhengce de Lilunkuangjia [New Structural Economics: A Framework for Rethinking Development and Policy]," Trans. Su Jian, Peking University Press, 2012; Justin Yifu Lin, "Fanrong de Qiusuo: Fazhanzhongjingji Ruhe Jueqi [The Quest for Prosperity: How Developing Economies Can Take Off]," Trans. Zhang Jianhua, Peking University Press, 2012. Justin Yifu Lin, "Xinjiegou Jingjixue Wenji [New Structural Economics Anthology]," Truth and Wisdom Press, Shanghai People's Press, 2012.

experience offers an academic foundation for the study of modern economics.

But how can the government guarantee that the industries they identify really have a comparative advantage? To answer this question, we must understand the operation of the economic system. In China's case, we must interpret its current economy system correctly. It has not been paid much attention, because some mainstream economists viewed it as a temporary system and will ultimately transfer to a conventional western-style system.

Among the little research that has been conducted, US-based Chinese scholars Professor Qian Yingyi and Professor Xu Chenggang first raised the theory of the Chinese government's M-form structure, it is decentralized local governments that under leadership of central government that promote the development of non-state economy and horizontal market relationships.[2] Later, Professor Qian Yingyi cooperated with Professor Barry Weingast of Stanford University in elevating the idea of decentralization to a theory of market-preserving federalism, which stressed the importance of institutionalizing the division of central and local powers.[3] But they did not directly analyze China's M-form structure or how the system of market-preserving federalism actually operated. A number of other scholars conducted empirical research into the influence of decentralization on economic growth and infrastructure development, the urban–rural gap, and the promotion of government officials and expenditures. But they still did not really deal with the main topic of how the Chinese economic system operates.

---

[2] Qian Yingyi and Xu Chenggang, "Zhongguo de Jingjigaige Weishenme yu Zhongbutong — M-xing de Cengjizhi he Feiguoyoubumen de Jinru yu Kuozhang [Why China's Economic Reforms Differ: The M-Form Hierarchy and Entry/Expansion of the Non-State Sector]," reprinted from Qian Yingyi's "Xiandai Jingjixue yu Zhongguo Jingjigaige," China Renmin University Press, 2003.

[3] Qian Yingyi and Barry R. Weingast, "Zhongguo Tese de Weihu Shichang de Jingji Lianbangzhi [Market Preserving Federalism, Chinese-style]," reprinted from Qian Yingyi's "Xiandai Jingjixue yu Zhongguo Jingjigaige," China Renmin University Press, 2003.

Professor Steven N. S. Cheung's book, "The Economic System of China," made a key breakthrough on this topic.[4] According to Professor Cheung's theory, the Chinese economic system is based on competitive federalism, because regional competition was a means for development, with local governments actively involved in guiding and motivating businesses, while also providing land and support services. In this way, part of the government's revenue from enterprises was no longer just "tax," but in the economic sense, it was "rent." Maximizing the pursuit of taxes by the government has the biggest negative impact on the market operation, whereas seeking rent just improves the efficiency in allocating resources and the level of market operation. Using this modern economic theory to explain the operation of China's economy offered a completely new paradigm.

This book attempts to expand Professor Cheung's theory, and through investigating the key fact that the local governments now operates as a market unit to reveal its influence on government behavior, market operation and macroeconomic performance. In the process, we will explain the institutional support behind China's supernormal economic growth and provide a basis for addressing the question of screening for viable businesses as proposed in Professor Lin's theory of New Structural Economics.

China's supernormal growth can be analyzed from two main perspectives: (i) institutional arrangements and (ii) the operation of the economy. The following discussion will be conducted from the perspective of the operation of the economy.

Starting from reform and opening up, China's economic growth has exhibited two conspicuous features. First, the unprecedented rate of growth. On the one hand, this period of fast-paced growth has already lasted 34 years and many economists are predicting that it will continue until at least 2030. So in total, this period of high growth may last for more than 50 years. This record would surpass anything

---

[4] This important research has already been included in a collection of essays edited by Zhang Jun and Zhou Lian, "Weizengzhang er Jingzheng: Zhongguo Zengzhang de Zhengzhijingjixue," Truth and Wisdom Press, Shanghai People's Press, 2008.

seen elsewhere in the world. On the other hand, during this 34-year time period, the growth rate was highest. According to the National Bureau of Statistics of China, the average gross domestic product (GDP) between 1978 and 2011 was 9.98%, with per capita GDP reaching 8.80%.[5] Even though the World Bank heralded the economies of Japan and other East Asian nations as "miracles," the growth in those countries never reached the heights achieved in China.[6]

Second, China's growth rate has clearly been more stable than in other countries. In the 34 years since reform and opening up, not only has the rate of economic expansion surpassed that in conventional economies, the cyclical fluctuations have also been significantly fewer. In fact, supernormal growth and super-low fluctuations are intimately linked. From the data, we can see that excessive economic volatility will inevitably drag down average growth. Similarly, in high-growth economies, as fluctuations increase, they can lead to a slowdown. China has been able to achieve supernormal economic expansion while experiencing only relatively low levels of volatility, further highlighting the uniqueness of its growth history.

While partly due to a favorable external environment, overcoming the cyclical volatility common in conventional economies and still experiencing supernormal growth can mainly be attributed to the formation of a unique socialist market economy, which itself was a product of reform and opening up and the creation of a new institutional system. Under this system, the market and central and local governments

---

[5] National Statistics Bureau of China, "China Statistical Yearbook 2012," China Statistics Press, 2012.

[6] Average annual GDP in Korea 1963–2002 — 7.998%; Singapore 1961–1997 — 8.635%; Japan 1950–1973 — 8.92%; Taiwan, China 1962–1994 — 9.03%; Hong Kong 1962–1988 — 8.626%. Data from IMF, "International Financial Statistics," 1983, 1985, 1996, 1997; "World Economic Outlook Database," April 2007; "Zhongguo Taiwan Jingji Jihua he Fazhanweiyuanhui: Taiwan Tongji Ziliao Shouce 2007 [State Development Planning Commission's Taiwan Statistical Handbook 2007 Taiwan]," reprinted from "Gaige Niandai de Jingji Zengzhang yu Jiegou Bianqian," Liu Xiahui, Zhang Ping and Zhang Xiaojing, Truth and Wisdom Press, Shanghai People's Press, 2008, p. 87.

were basically interwoven, acting together to produce sustained supernormal investment. The exploration of the relationship between China's government and the market has afforded a major breakthrough in terms of the study of standard economic theory.

1. Supernormal Growth

The unconventional nature of China's economic expansion was first reflected in the high average annual growth rates, which never happened before.[7] There are some scholars who harbor doubts about the nature of China's growth. They say there have been many countries that over a long enough time period have experienced fast-paced economic expansion. Others have said that it was simply the result of favorable international economic conditions, an argument that trivializes the difficulties experienced in achieving such high growth. In order to address these misgivings, we must examine and analyze China's experience within a comparative historical framework. At this point, we should highlight the concept of "the basic stage of national industrialization." The reason for this is to illustrate, first, that as a country goes through different stages of development, the economic growth rate will change. Second, we must clearly distinguish between the countries that developed first and those that came after. Those who developed later could introduce technology from the more advanced countries and emulate their experience, possibly increasing the pace of their own development (Table 1.1). In the history of growth in modern economics, the United Kingdom was the global pioneer, being the country where the First Industrial Revolution began. In the Second Industrial Revolution, the US took England's place, becoming the world leader in technological progress and economic expansion. Throughout this process, the United States along with the United Kingdom and its associated countries including Canada, New Zealand and Australia, all leapt into the ranks of developed nations.

[7] National Statistics Bureau of China, "China Statistical Yearbook 2012," China Statistics Press, 2012.

Table 1.1 Average GDP Growth Rates During Industrialization

Country	Stage of industrialization	Time period	Average annual GDP growth rate (%)	Per capita GDP growth rate (%)
UK	Pioneer	1820–1870	2.05	1.26
US	Follow-up/pioneer	1870–1913	4.04	1.82
Japan (1)	Catch-up	1950–1973	8.92	7.70
Japan (2)	Catch-up	1950–1984	7.20	6.09
India	Catch-up	1990–2011	6.47	4.66
China	Catch-up	1978–2011	9.98	8.80

Source: UK and US data from "Shijie Jingji Qiannianshi [*The World Economy: a Millennial Perspective by* Angus Maddison]," Trans. Wu Xiaoying, Peking University Press, 2003; Japanese data uses 1990 as a baseline reference and taken from "Historical Statistics of Japan — Gross Domestic Product Classified by Economic Activities — 68SNA"; Indian data from IMF "World Economic and Financial Surveys," October 2012; China data from the National Bureau of Statistics, "China Statistical Yearbook," China Statistics Press, 2012.

After the Second World War, Japan, as well as the so-called Four Asian Tigers of Singapore, South Korea, Taiwan and Hong Kong, adopted a catch-up strategy, thereby experiencing comparatively long periods of high growth and becoming high-income economies. Finally, amid the wave of globalization in recent decades, many emerging economies have experienced good economic growth, with India being a fine example and worth looking at more closely. We will choose several representative nations to compare with China.

Clearly, the later the countries developed, the faster they pushed through the industrialization stage. The United Kingdom was the first country to undergo this process, but by comparing its pace of average growth with today's standards, it appears quite low, at only 2.05%. China's growth rate for more than 30 years was more than four times stronger. The backward countries, including the US, Canada, New Zealand and Australia, all benefited from their ability to copy and import from the United Kingdom's experience and consequently their growth rates during industrialization were noticeably higher. Indeed, by 1906, GDP in the US had surpassed that of the United Kingdom, becoming the leading world economy.[8] However, throughout this time, US annual growth was only 4%. By comparison, during the same period of development in China, the growth rate was roughly 2.5 times as fast. In Japan, after 1950, the economy experienced 20 to 30 years of high growth with US scholars proclaiming "Japan as Number One" and the World Bank heralding it as the Asian Miracle.[9]

But even Japan's record of fast-paced growth was lower than China's. Take the short period from 1950 to 1973 as an example: its average per capita GDP growth only managed to get within 1.1 percentage point of China's (7.70% versus 8.80%). However, as Japan's economy began to slow after 1974, per capita growth between 1950 and 1984 was 6.09%, 3 percentage points behind China. In 1984, the Japanese economy contracted even further, entering a prolonged period of downturn. If we compare the period from 1950 to 2010, the difference is even more pronounced. We can make the same comparison with India, another developing country. From the start of the 1990s, when reform began, the growth rate greatly accelerated, averaging 6% between 1990 and 2011, joining China to become one of the BRICS (the five major emerging nations of Brazil, Russia, India, China and South Africa). But still, China's growth was on average 3.51 percentage points higher. So it is clear that regardless of which stage of development China is compared with in other leading countries, the growth seen during its period of industrialization was still higher.

Below, we will use Japan and India for examples. After the Second World War, Japan's economy soared. But in fact, the economy had been gradually modernizing since the beginning of the Meiji restoration period and by the time the Second World War began Japan's level of industrialization was already considerable. During the war, Japan engaged in fierce combat with us navy by domestically-made aircraft carrier and fighter planes, and at the

---

[8] US per capita GDP exceeded that of the UK in 1906. Robert Gordon, "Is US Economic Growth Over? Faltering Innovation Confronts 2010", NBER Working Paper Series, 2011.

[9] Ezra Vogel, "Riben Minglie Diyi: Dui Meiguo de Jiaoxun [Japan as Number One: Lessons for America]," Trans. Gu Ying, World Affairs Press, 1980.

same time deadlocked with China and Southeast Asia, revealing its industrial power. In the early postwar period, Japan, as a defeated nation, experienced negative growth and struggled in plight. However, the subsequent outbreak of the Korean War spurred Japanese exports. Later, America started to support Japan for geostrategic purpose. Adding most of Japan's manufacturing sector was preserved and the aggregation of human capital and management still functioned well, Japan recovered quickly from the war and entered the sustainable and rapid development.[10]

Studying Japan's high period of growth between 1950 and 1973 before the oil crisis, it is easy to see many similarities with China's own economic expansion following reform and opening up. First, there were favorable conditions in international markets. And not only did the US provide Japan with more than US$2 billion in economic aid, but it also opened up its domestic market. Additionally, as market forces came into play, Japan's Ministry of International Trade and Industry instigated an export-oriented growth strategy, taking advantage of low international commodity prices to promote processing trade. Subsequent upgrades transitioned the industrial structure from labor-intensive manufacturing to heavy industry. After the oil crisis and against a backdrop of soaring raw material prices, heavy industry was further transitioned to vehicle manufacturing, electronics, semiconductors and other technology-intensive industries. However, after Japan racked up a massive trade surplus and the US recorded a trade deficit, the government came under tremendous pressure from Washington to let the yen appreciate. This resulted in the signing of the Plaza Accord and led to unprecedented asset bubbles with the Japanese economy remaining mired in a slump since 1990.[11] This

[10] Nakamura Takafusa, ed., "Riben Jingjishi: Di 7 Juan [Economic History of Japan; Volume 7]," Trans. Hu Qilin, Hu Jing, Lin Hua, Joint Publishing, 1997; Yasukichi Yasuba, Inoki Takenori, ed., "Riben Jingjishi: Di 8 Juan [Economic History of Japan; Volume 8]," Trans. Lian Xiang, Joint Publishing, 1997; Kobayashi Yoshio, "Zhanhou Riben Jingjishi [Post-War Economic History of Japan]," Trans. Sun Hanchao and Ma Junlei, The Commercial Press, 1985.

[11] For further reading on bubbles in the Japanese economy, see Richard Koo, "Dashuaitui — Ruhe zai Jinrong Weijizhong Xincun he Fazhan [The Holy Grail of

illustrated the close link between Japan's post-war fast-paced growth and the comparatively forceful actions of the state in the economy, with scholars branding the concept as the Developmental State.[12]

However, it should be pointed out that after the yen was allowed to appreciate, the economy experienced a bubble and became ensnared in a long period of stagnation. China, on the other hand, was able to gradually defuse the pressure on the renminbi to appreciate, opening up the prospect for long-term sustainable growth. The reason was that there were significant structural differences between China's socialist market economy and Japan's Developmental State model. So even if we compare China's growth since reform and opening up with Japan's economy over the long-term, it would still be considered supernormal.

Of course, the most meaningful reference for comparison with China is India. Both countries have a long history of civilization, similar sized populations and large land areas. And although over the past 100 years or more, both economies experienced development at their own pace, by the end of the 1970s, there was not much separating the two levels of economic progress. In the wave of globalization, they also both conducted market-oriented reforms. The difference was that India enacted a democratic parliamentary system and had a comparatively higher level of privatization.[13] Economic reform in China started at the end of the 1970s, before India, where it did not begin until the early 1990s. So the differences between the two countries' growth was more pronounced in the beginning. Looking at Table 1.2, if we compare India's period of highest growth, which was from 1994 onwards, we can see that the average rate in China was 10.08%, 3.11

Macro Economics: Lessons from Japan's Great Recession]," Trans. Yu Haixiang, The Eastern Publishing Company, 2008.

[12]For further reading on the Japanese government's functions, see Chalmers Johnson, "MITI and the Japanese Miracle: The Growth of Industrial Policy, 1925–1975," Stanford, CA: Standford University Press, 1982; For further reading on developmental states, see Meredith Woo-Cummins, ed., "Fazhanxing Guojia [The Developmental State]," Trans. Cao Haijun, Jilin Publishing Group, 2008.

[13]Montek S. Ahluwalia, "Economic Reforms in India since 1991: Has Gradualism Worked?" *Journal of Economic Perspectives*, Vol. 16, 2002.

percentage points higher than India's 6.97%. This further shows that China's economic growth has been supernormal.

2. Super-low Economic Volatility

One of the main reasons for China's high growth rate since reform and opening up is that in the past 20 years, the economy has managed to avoid cyclical market volatility. In studying the process of economic development, we cannot just look at the growth in GDP and per capita GDP, we must also examine the stability of economic expansion and the extent of cyclical volatility.

In a market economy, the business cycle usually is accompanied by periods of boom, recession, depression and then recovery. The pace of long periods of growth is dependent on the stability of the expansion or growth over the majority of the time, and not just one-off exceptions or growth over only a few years. To measure the stability of growth, we can use three types of indicators: (1) *Range of variation.* The difference between the highest GDP growth rate and the lowest will show us the maximum range of variation across different years. (2) *Standard deviation.* The deviation from the average growth rate can be used to show the extent of volatility during a certain period. The larger the standard deviation, the higher the level of volatility. (3) *Relative standard deviation.* If we take the standard deviation divided by the average growth rate, we can use it to show the relative economic volatility. The larger the figure, the larger the economic fluctuation. So it is evident that high economic growth and low volatility have been intimately linked in the process of China's expansion since reform and opening up. This can be highlighted when comparing the different stages of growth.

In Figure 1.1, we can see that from 1978, China's economy overall maintained relatively stable and consistent growth. However, there were three years when extraordinary circumstances affected the economy and it slowed (in 1981, during a period of re-adjustment, growth was only 5%; 1989 and 1990 were

Table 1.2 Real GDP Growth Rates in China and India: 1978–2011

Year	China's real GDP growth (%)	India's real GDP growth (%)	Year	China's real GDP growth (%)	India's real GDP growth (%)
1978	11.67		**1994**	13.08	6.20
1979	7.57		**1995**	10.92	7.35
1980	7.84	3.63	**1996**	10.01	7.56
1981	5.24	6.18	**1997**	9.30	4.62
1982	9.06	4.07	**1998**	7.83	5.99
1983	10.85	6.37	**1999**	7.62	6.90
1984	15.18	4.65	**2000**	8.43	5.71
1985	13.47	4.89	**2001**	8.30	3.89
1986	8.85	4.88	**2002**	9.08	4.56
1987	11.58	4.15	**2003**	10.03	6.85
1988	11.28	8.26	**2004**	10.09	7.59
1989	4.06	6.81	**2005**	11.31	9.04
1990	3.84	5.63	**2006**	12.68	9.53
1991	9.18	2.14	**2007**	14.16	10.00
1992	14.24	4.39	**2008**	9.63	6.90
1993	13.96	4.94	**2009**	9.21	5.88
			2010	10.45	10.09
			2011	9.29	6.84
Average	9.87	5.07	**Average**	10.08	6.97
Maximum	15.18	8.26	**Maximum**	14.16	10.09
Minimum	3.84	2.14	**Minimum**	7.62	3.89
Standard Deviation	3.73	1.51	**Standard Deviation**	1.80	1.81
Relative standard deviation (%)	37.64	29.80	**Relative standard deviation (%)**	17.84	26.01

Note: *Standard deviation*: the square root of the value of the squared deviation from the mean. *Relative standard deviation*: divide standard deviation by the mean then multiply the result by 100%.

Source: China data from the National Bureau of Statistics, "China Statistical Yearbook," China Statistics Press, 2012. India data from IMF, "World Economic and Financial Surveys," October 2012.

Figure 1.1 China's Real GDP Growth: 1978–2011 (%).

Source: National Statistics Bureau of China, "China Statistical Yearbook 2012," China Statistics Press, 2012.

affected by political upheaval and growth slowed to 4.06% and 3.84%, respectively). Apart from those years, growth in other periods was over 6%. Compared with before reform and opening up, economic volatility in the period after was much improved.[14] It is easy to see the special significance of the growth in the middle and later stages of the 1990s. In 1992, it reached a peak of 14.24% and then began to decline right through to 1999, when it reached a low of 7.62%. Over seven years, growth declined on average by 1 percentage point a year. From then on, it was a straight upward climb, rebounding to 14.16% in 2007 and even managing to hold above 9% in 2008 despite the impact of the global economic crisis. This continued all the way through to 2011. Simply put, following the period of transition from 1992 to 1999, China's economy steered a course of high growth from 2000 to 2011 during which time average expansion basically held above 9%. This is a very rare phenomenon and we are yet to fully explore the meaning behind it.

[14] Liu Xiahui, Zhang Ping and Zhang Xiaojing, "Gaige Niandai de Jingji Zengzhang yu Jiegou Bianqian," Truth and Wisdom Press, Shanghai People's Press, 2008.

It is worth highlighting that this period of sustained economic boom corresponded with the forming and completion of the structure for China's socialist market economy. Deng Xiaoping's "Southern Tour" in 1992 brought about a new wave of economic reform and development with growth exceeding 10% for five consecutive years. However, throughout this time, the dual-track pricing system still widely existed, while the institutional basis that guarantees the long-term stable economic growth had not been accomplished yet. At the same time, with low levels of productivity already causing a serious surplus of production capacity, it was commonly believed among domestic economists that China had transformed from a "shortage economy" to a "surplus economy."[15] It was against this backdrop that in 1992, the central government established the goals for the reform of the socialist market economic system at the 14th National Congress of the Communist Party of China after clashes between theorists and much ideological emancipation.[16]

In November 1993, during the third plenary session of the Central Committee of the Communist Party of China, "The Decision on Issues Concerning the Establishment of a Socialist Market Economic System," was adopted. Centered around the goal of establishing a socialist market system were a number of other coordinated plans and initiatives to promote the reform.[17] The most important

[15] Shortage economics is concept conceived by a Hungarian economist Janos Kornai (1986) addressing the Soviet-style planned economic system. It emphasizes how all goods were commonly in shortage under the Soviet system. By the early 1990s as China was in the initial stages of market reform, there were cases whereby there were shortages of some products and a surplus of others, attracting widespread attention in academia.

[16] Ling Zhijun's work under the title "Jiaofeng [Crossing Swords]" is a complete and accurate account of the confrontation of ideas at the time. See also Ma Licheng and Ling Zhijun, "Jiaofeng: Dangdai Zhongguo Sanci Sixiang Jiefang Shilu [Crossing Swords — A Record of Three Periods of Ideological Liberation in Contemporary China]," Hubei People's Press, 2008.

[17] For further reading on the problems of reform after 1993, see Wu Jinglian's "Dangdai Zhongguo Jingji Gaige," Shanghai Far East Press, 2004, pp. 70–81. "Wu Jinglian: Zixuenji 1980–2003," Shanxi Economic Press, 2003, pp. 156–189.

of which included accelerating the pace of market reform, introduction of the tax sharing system and decentralization, which categorized central and regional taxes, the strategic restructuring of major state-owned enterprises and the reorganization of a large number of small-and-medium-sized state-owned businesses. Also included was reform of the foreign exchange regime and foreign exchange controls. All of these initiatives were conducted right up until China's entry into the World Trade Organization in 2001.

This series of major reforms overcame serious difficulties and in a relatively short period of time were put into place one after the other. If we use China's entry into the World Trade Organization as a benchmark, by the beginning of the 21st century, the basic framework of the socialist market economy had taken shape. Under this market system, companies became comparatively independent, managing their own business and making their own self-seeking plans for development amid this new market microcosm. Local governments besides enterprises, to some extent, became another market subject to pursue regional development. Thus, Chinese-style market which consist of enterprises, local governments and central government became basic force of resource allocation and put the economy on track for continued high, fast-paced growth. After booming economic growth between 1992 and 1994, the Chinese economy experienced a soft landing, withstanding the impact of the 1997 Asian financial crisis and steering toward a new round of growth. In fact, overall, except for the two years after the Asian crisis, when growth dipped slightly under 8% (7.83% in 1998 and 7.62% in 1999), the economy expanded at an average of more than 8% in the 17 years between 1994 and 2011.

It was during this period from 1994 up until the beginning of the 21st century, that China's socialist market economy was basically formed, greatly changing the shape of economic growth experienced since the 1978 policy of reform and opening up. The most important change was the nation's ability to maintain supernormal growth while at the same time greatly mitigating economic volatility. We can take 1994 as the pivotal year in which the socialist market economy and all its attendant reform policies were comprehensively implemented. The years after were when the system of a socialist market economy was formed and improved. The years prior to 1993 were the transition period from the traditional planned economy.

Table 1.3 demonstrates the huge differences of economic growth pattern in two periods. By comparing average annual growth rates between the years before 1994, when the economy was in transition as the new system went into operation, the difference in terms of average GDP was very little (9.87% and 10.08%). But when comparing the stability of economic growth, we can tell at a glance that the difference is very pronounced. During the transition stage between 1978 and 1993, there were no major external shocks. However, there were three significant dips in 1981, 1986 and 1990, with average growth falling from 15.18 to 3.84% between 1984 and 1990. The largest variance blew out to 11.34 percentage points, so it cannot be said there were not ups and downs. But the operation of the socialist market mechanism enabled the national economy to avoid the massive fluctuations caused by the external shocks of the 1997 Asian financial crisis and the 2008 global financial crisis. Between 1994 and 2011, the fastest growth rate was 14.16% in 2007 and the slowest was 7.62% in 1999, a variance of only 6.54 percentage points. The standard deviation between these two periods, 1978 to 1993, is 3.73, more than double the 1.8 experienced between 1994 and 2011.

Table 1.3 Comparison Between Two Periods in China's Economic Growth: 1978–2011

	1978–1993	**1994–2011**
Average GDP growth rate (%)	9.87	10.08
Highest growth rate (%)	15.18	14.16
Lowest growth rate (%)	3.84	7.62
Variance	11.34	6.54
Standard deviation	3.73	1.80
Relative standard deviation (%)	37.64	17.84

Source: Calculations are based on data from National Statistics Bureau of China, "China Statistical Yearbook 2012," China Statistics Press, 2012.

From this data, it is obvious that China's supernormal growth rate and extremely low economic volatility are closely related. Whether the average long-term economic growth rate is high or low is not dependent on the elevated levels seen in just a few years, but determined by calculating all of the years with high or low growth. Even after more than 30 years of successful operation, the Chinese economy is still functioning at a very high level. This has been especially evident in the years since 1994, with even the lowest growth rate still coming in higher than 7%. Imagine if it were the period before the reforms and opening up, the highs would surge to over 20% and the lows would plunge to negative growth and average economic expansion would not be high. Therefore, the most direct explanation of the reasons behind China's growth since reform and opening up is that its economic cycles are different. The key to supernormal expansion has been overcoming and resolving the cyclical fluctuations that face conventional economic growth models, resulting in long-term, high-performance operation of the system and uninterrupted fast-paced growth.

We can compare the economic fluctuations in China and India to illustrate this point. From Table 1.2, we can see there is a difference between the average growth rates and the extent of volatility in the Chinese economy is clearly less than that of India. Although economic reform in India has lifted the country's average growth rate, it has not been able to avoid the cyclical fluctuations commonly observed in market economies as China has done.

India's economic reforms were started slightly before those of China's socialist market economy had come into full swing in 1994. Between 1994 and 2011, India's average GDP grew from 5.07% seen between 1980 and 1993 to 6.97%, clearly showing the effect that reforms had on lifting the pace of growth. But after 1994, the degree of economic fluctuations had not improved. The stark differences between the economies of India and China become clear when looking at how each weathered the impact of the Asian financial crisis in 1997 and the global financial crisis in 2008. After the 1997 crisis, China's economic growth only dipped below 8% in 1998 and 1999, before returning to over 8% in 2000 and then maintaining high growth thereafter. India, on the other hand, experienced six years of major economic volatility, with GDP in 1997 falling from more than 7% to 4.62%. It went on to tumble to a low of 3.89% in 2001 and by 2003 had only managed to recover to over 6%. Similarly, after the global financial crisis, India's growth rate tumbled to less than 6%, while China's held above 9%. We can see that regardless of whether we compare its ability to resist the shock of a financial crisis or its recovery, China's economy is stronger than that of India.

In examining the statistics, because the average growth rates between China and India are different, we should use the relative standard deviation, not the standard deviation, to measure the differences in volatility between the two economies. Relative standard deviation measures economic fluctuations as a percentage relative to the average, so during periods of clearly different levels of volatility between two economies, relative standard deviation is the most objective indicator. Considering the overall data in the last 30 years or more, India's relative standard deviation for economic growth and volatility significantly exceeded that of China.

If we take 1993 as the demarcation point between the two time periods of pre-1993 and post-1993, we see that the difference in economic volatility between China and India is even bigger. Between 1978 and 1993, China's growth rate exceeded India's, but the volatility was also relatively higher (during this period, China's relative standard deviation was 37.64% and between 1980 and 1993, India's was 29.8%, a variance of almost 8 percentage points). But the situation changed after 1994, with China's socialist market economic system again lifting the average GDP growth rate and also greatly increasing the stability of the expansion. From 1994 to 2011, the relative standard deviation of China's economic growth dropped by almost 20 percentage points to 17.84%, while India's only dropped slightly to 26.01%. China's economic volatility had dropped from being almost 8 percentage points higher than India's to 8 percentage points lower, a massive achievement. From this, we can infer that prior to 1994, the socialist market economic system was not yet in place and could not offset market slumps. But after 1994, with the formation of the system, the cyclical downward forces that are commonly seen in market economies had been effectively eliminated, while India had yet to significantly improve. Thus, while the sustainability of India's economic development remained as it had been in the past, China had totally surpassed the market norm and achieved supernormal growth.

3. Fast-paced Consumption Growth and Increased Efficiency

China's fast-paced economic growth brought with it the rapid increase in the level of consumption and a continued improvement in economic efficiency. Currently, society and media both commonly attribute the supernormal growth of China's economy to high levels of investment, high waste and low consumption, which is a misconception. In reality, in the past 34 years of economic development, high growth in GDP, investment and consumption all occurred in unison. In Table 1.1 and Table A.1 in the appendix, we can see that between 1978 and 2011, China's average growth rate was 9.98%, annual investment grew 10.92% and consumption expanded 9.15%. Even total per capita consumption growth reached the annual rate of 8.05%. In the past 34 years, to have reached per capita consumption growth of 8.05% is a unique achievement in world economic history.

Why do so many people attribute the success of China's economy to low consumption? Maybe it is because they confuse the contribution of consumption to GDP with the level of consumption. To be sure, the contribution of consumption to GDP is comparatively low, reaching an average of 59.56% throughout the entire 34-year timeframe in question, while in Western market economies, the usual figure is over 75%. But low contribution to GDP does not equal low levels of consumption. In fact, the contrary is true, as a low consumption ratio indicates that investment levels are high (capital formation) and the scale of investment is large, which consequently brings higher GDP growth. If the consumption ratio is low under conditions of rapid GDP growth, then there is a good chance that it could also rise quickly. Imagine for a moment that if over the past 34 years, consumption and investment as percentages of GDP were the same ratios as they are in conventional economies, that is, over 75% for consumption and under

25% for investment, what would be the outcome? First, annual growth would fall to a level comparable to or slightly higher than that in India. Perhaps, 7.5% and 2012 GDP would not be more than RMB51 trillion, but instead only about RMB25 trillion. The level of consumption would not be the current rate of RMB30 trillion (which is the RMB51 trillion GDP figure multiplied by a consumption ratio of 59.56%) and would instead fall to RMB18.75 trillion (RMB25 trillion multiplied by a consumption ratio of over 75%). That is, comparatively low consumption and high investment bring about rapid increases in the level of consumption, while high consumption and low investment rates cause long-term low consumption levels. This is the dialectic relationship between investment, growth and consumption.

The problem is that high rates of investment come with risk: if it does not bring high growth and instead leads to overproduction and economic crisis, the result can be enormous waste, which is a major problem. China has succeeded in unleashing the market's special economic advantages and strategically exploited the extraordinary buying power of the international community to avoid large-scale overproduction, while maintaining high levels of economic operation and supernormal growth. Because of this, throughout the entire process of achieving supernormal growth, investment efficiency was quite normal and labor productivity jumped. We know that the composite indicator to measure the efficiency of investment is the capital–output ratio, which shows the amount of investment required for every unit of GDP growth. Table 1.4 shows the capital–output ratios for China, the US and Japan.

China's capital–output ratio in the 33 years between 1978 and 2010 was 4.03. Between 1978 and 1987, it was 3.38 and from 2001 to 2010, it was 4.10. What does this indicator mean? In a horizontal comparison, in the US, the ratio between 1965 and 2010 was 5.29 and in Japan between 1980 and 2010, it was 14.69. We can see that China's investment efficiency in the era of reform was comparatively higher. In a vertical comparison, China's capital–output ratio rose from 3.38 in the early stages to 4.10 more recently, meaning that for every RMB1 of GDP growth, an investment of

Table 1.4 Capital–Output Ratios of China, the US and Japan

Country	Year	GDP growth	Investment growth	Capital–output ratio
China (RMB 100 million)	1978–1987	35,105.20	118,702.49	3.381
	1988–1997	85,311.24	332,508.47	3.898
	1998–2007	230,625.46	871,342.94	3.778
	2001–2010	311,806.99	1,277,713.49	4.098
	1978–2010	**469,751.29**	**1,894,447.34**	4.032
US (US$1 billion)	1965–1974	1,268.40	5,207.20	4.105
	1975–1984	1,968.00	7,229.60	3.674
	1985–1994	2,242.60	10,014.50	4.466
	1995–2004	3,977.00	17,198.30	4.324
	2005–2009	440.00	9,961.50	22.640
	1965–2010	**9,692.10**	**51,269.10**	**5.290**
Japan (1 billion yen)	1980–1989	154,660.38	966,275.52	6.248
	1990–1999	50,352.95	1,301,008.18	25.838
	2000–2010	33,069.60	1,228,984.64	37.164
	1980–2010	**238,082.93**	**3,496,268.34**	**14.685**

Note: In the calculation of the capital–output ratio, it is difficult to measure when investments will produce beneficial results. To simplify matters, we will use the total investment for the 10-year period and the increase in the one-year lag total for 10-year GDP figure to calculate the average 10-year capital–output ratio. There are other ways to calculate the capital–output ratio, but here we are concerned with an economy's overall performance over a comparatively long period.

Source: China data from the National Statistics Bureau, "China Statistical Yearbook 2012," China Statistics Press, 2012. The real GDP and investment data assume 2012 as the base year for constant prices.

US data from BEA, "GDP and Other Major NIPA Series, 1929–2012: II," August 2012. Real GDP and investment data assume 2005 as the base year for constant prices.

Japanese data from the IMF, "World Economic Outlook Database," October 2012. Real GDP assumes 2005 as the base year for constant prices. Actual investment was derived by multiplying the investment rate by the GDP at constant prices.

For more detailed data, see Tables A.2–A.4 in the appendix.

RMB4.10 is now required, compared to RMB3.38 previously. The investment amount required for every unit of GDP growth had increased considerably.

How can this be explained? And can we assume that China's investment efficiency will decline? If we view this through the common theory of economic development, this will not be the case. That is because as a nation's industrialization deepens, light industry gives way to heavy industry. Karl Marx in his work "Das Kapital" put forward the principle of the organic composition of capital[18] in which the ratio of constant capital such as factory buildings, equipment, materials and other manufacturing components will continually increase, while the ratio of variable capital such as labor force will constantly fall. Therefore, the share of capital goods in total social output will increase and the share of consumer goods will fall.

After Marx proposed his theory on capital accumulation, there were discussions of a similar nature among Western economists. But while Marx said capital would organically increase, it was now proposed that capital-intensive technology would replace labor-intensive technology. Today, the increase in the organic composition of capital, or the rise in the proportion of capital goods, serves as an objective historical economic law, and reflects the process of the Second Industrial Revolution as a historical trend. With the advent of the information revolution and the rise of tertiary industries, the structure of investment and consumption in the socialist economy underwent change again, with the share of consumption gradually increasing and that of investment gradually declining. This has emerged in China over the past two years.

In short, China's investment efficiency over the last 34 years has been pretty good overall, and certainly better than in the US and Japan. The slight increase in the capital–output ratio reflected the objective laws of industrialization. Thus, large-scale sustained investment results in the basis for revolutionary changes to the entire social infrastructure and a huge increase in labor productivity.

In Figure 1.2, from 1978 to 2011, China's labor productivity jumped from RMB5,400 per person to RMB64,300, a roughly

[18] See Karl Marx, "Zibenlun: Di 1 Juan Di 7 Pian [Das Kapital]," People's Publishing House, 2004.

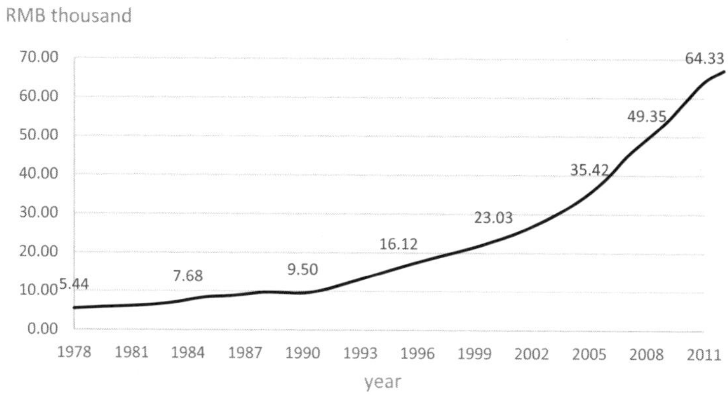

Figure 1.2 The Increase in Labor's Productivity of China: 1978–2011.

Note: Labor productivity rate is calculated by dividing the real GDP by employment, whereas the employment figures from 1979, 1981–1984 and 1986–1989 were estimates. Base year: 2012.
Source: China data from the National Statistics Bureau, "China Statistical Yearbook 2012," China Statistics Press, 2012.

12-fold increase. Although China's abundant supply of labor was a demographic dividend for economic growth, the "efficiency dividend" highlighted by the increase in labor productivity was the really astonishing thing.

4. The Periodic Crises of Market Economy

The above analysis shows that China's economy had actually made the coexistence of extraordinary achievement of high investment, high growth and high consumption all at the same time possible. The direct cause of this can be attributed to the emergence of the national economy operating at a high level over a long period and avoiding the periodic crises from which are inevitable in conventional economies.

But why is China able to have avoided cyclical economic volatility during the prolonged economic growth after 1994? To answer this, we must first clarify: why do conventional economies experience cyclical fluctuations?

Looking at the classical theories of political economists, we can explain the business cycle from supply side and demand side.[19]

First, we will examine it from the supply side. Once the economy is operating normally, investment and demand growth should boost the other, naturally leading to an increase in the pace of economic growth and leading to a period of prosperity. This is a natural phenomenon within the market operation. But once the peak of economic prosperity has been reached, the level of industry profits begins to decline. The reasons are thus: (1) in times of economic prosperity, increased investment follows, leading to expanded manufacturing capacity; increased capacity leads to a rise in the price of capital goods, causing higher investment costs and falling returns; (2) times of prosperity also mean that the economy is overheated, which causes the price of daily necessities to rise and at the same time an increase in demand for labor leading to an increase in wages. The result of all this is a rise in the costs of manufacturing and a decline in profits.

Examining this theory from the demand side, we can see that periods of prosperity are when wages rise the quickest and subsequently consumption increases. According to Keynes' theory of the marginal propensity to consume, during these times, consumption tends to fall. This is because rising income spurs increased consumption, but the proportion of new income used for consumption will be lower than the original ratio. This shows that increases in

---

[19] The study of the general theory of economic cycles includes the differing views of Marx, Friedrich August Hayek and John Maynard Keynes. The issue addressed whether short periods of economic volatility are experienced every three to five years does not include factors like major reforms in technology that may cause long economic cycles, such as the so-called Kondratiev waves. The brief explanation of economic cycles in this book mainly referenced the following translated works: Karl Marx, "Zibenlun: Di 1 Juan Di 7 Pian [Das Kapital]," People's Publishing House, 2004; Friedrich August Hayek, "Wujia yu Shengchan [Prices and Production]," Shanghai People's Press, 1958; John Maynard Keynes, "[Jiuye, Lixi yu Huobi Tonglun [The General Theory Of Employment, Interest, And Money]," China Social Sciences Press, 2009.

consumption will be slower than the pace of income increases, with the proportion of income being saved rising. The scale of savings will in turn rise faster than that of income.

To sum up, during periods of prosperity, on the demand side, savings rise and consumption falls as there is a lack of consumer demand. On the supply side, precisely as costs rise, profits fall. Therefore, investment sentiment weakens, causing a trend whereby savings greatly outweigh investment and there is a lack of investment demand. The end result of this is that overall demand is less than overall supply. A booming economy expands production causing overproduction and supply of products is greater than demand. Prices drop and deflation occurs, leading the economy to swing from prosperity to decline and crisis.

Of course in times of boom, it is common that the expansion of credit may delay the onset of economic decline, but in the end, the banking system will face pressure in recovering their loans. So at best, this can only delay economic decline, but it cannot prevent it. Additionally, the greater the expansion of credit, the greater the economic decline will be when it comes. Frederick Engels summarized it concisely as follows:

> *Since 1825, when the first general crisis broke out, the whole industrial and commercial world, production and exchange among all civilized peoples and their more or less barbaric hangers-on, are thrown out of joint about once every 10 years. Commerce is at a stand-still, the markets are glutted, products accumulate, as multitudinous as they are unsaleable, hard cash disappears, credit vanishes, factories are closed, the mass of the workers are in want of the means of subsistence, because they have produced too much of the means of subsistence; bankruptcy follows upon bankruptcy, execution upon execution. The stagnation lasts for years; productive forces and products are wasted and destroyed wholesale, until the accumulated mass of commodities finally filter off, more or less depreciated in value, until production and exchange gradually begin to move again. Little by little, the pace quickens. It becomes a trot. The industrial trot breaks into a canter, the canter in turn grows into the headlong gallop of a perfect steeplechase of industry, commercial credit, and speculation, which finally, after breakneck*

leaps, ends where it began — in the ditch of a crisis. And so over and over again.[20]

We can say that cyclical downturns are innate to market economies. Just as the UK Industrial Revolution brought the economies of America and Europe into the modern capitalist era, the economic cycles will continue to stubbornly persist. Table 1.5 shows some of the cycles in major market economies.

It is interesting to note that whenever a market economy has experienced comparatively long years of prosperity, there is always someone, whether it is a politician, scholar or commentator, who stands up and says this is the end of economic cycles. But every time not long after this short-sighted clamor, a crisis emerges

Table 1.5 Economic Cycles of Selected Major Market Economies

Country	Time period	Number of economic cycles	Years of economic crisis
UK	1816–1870	9	1816, 1819, 1826, 1832, 1837, 1840–1842, 1848, 1857, 1866
US	1870–1904	4	1873, 1882, 1893, 1903
Japan	1950–1973	3	1954–1958, 1965, 1971
	1974–1990	2	1974, 1980–1983
India	1990–2011	5	1990, 1997, 2001, 2009, 2011
China	1978–1993	3	1981, 1986, 1990
	1994–2012	0	—

Source: UK data from Broadberry and O'Rourke, The Cambridge Economic History of Modern Europe, Vol. I, pp. 1700–1870. US data from "Zhuyao Zibenzhuyiguojia Jingjijianshi," ed. Fan Kang, People's Publishing House, 2001. Japanese data from the Statistics Bureau of Japan, "Historical Statistics of Japan — Gross Domestic Product Classified by Economic Activities — 68SNA" with 1990 as the base year. Indian data from IMF, "World Economic and Financial Surveys," October 2012. China data from the National Statistics Bureau, "China Statistical Yearbook 2012," China Statistics Press, 2012.

[20] Frederick Engels, "Fandulinlun [Anti-Duhring]," reprinted from "Makesi Engesi Xuanji: Di 3 Juan [Marx and Engels Collected Works]" People's Publishing House, 1995, p. 626. Available at: http://www.marxists.org/archive/marx/works/1880/soc-utop/ch03.htm.

as if on schedule. The most recent example of this was at the beginning of the 21st century as the US economy's reliance on information technology and Federal Reserve Chairman Alan Greenspan's lose monetary policy resulted in eight years of strong economic growth, inspiring all kinds of blindly optimistic theories, among which the most prominent was that the new economy had heralded the disappearance of the business cycle. Subsequently, not long after in 2002, the Internet bubble burst and the NASDAQ crashed, tumbling from 5,048.62 to 1,108 in one stroke, sowing the seeds of the Fed's later expansion of credit to the real estate industry. This led to the subprime mortgage crisis and, in turn, the global financial crisis from which we are yet to recover.

Every time there is an economic crisis, it always destroys the existing social productivity. In the classical scenario of an economic crisis, the products of overcapacity are dumped in other markets or simply wasted. The excess manufacturing capacity is idled, destroyed or abandoned, creating the conditions for a new wave of growth. But with state intervention in a modern capitalist system, the combined forces of expansionary macroeconomic policies and the financial asset bubble greatly delayed the outbreak of crisis. The result is that when the bubble finally bursts and crisis erupts, the impact felt by society and the economy is even more severe. In the last 10 years, the US has seen the Internet bubble burst and the housing market collapse, leading to a truly appalling number of company collapses and scrapped industry investments. This is also the core reason why the investments of individual enterprises are effective and high capital–output ratios refuse to fall. When the bubble bursts, when industry declines, all of society suffers. Former White House budget director David A. Stockman writes in *The New York Times*:

> *Over the last 13 years, the stock market has twice crashed and touched off a recession: American households lost $5 trillion in the 2000 dot-com bust and more than $7 trillion in the 2007 housing crash. Sooner or later — within a few years, I predict — this latest Wall Street bubble, inflated by an egregious flood of phony money from the Federal Reserve rather than real*

> *economic gains, will explode, too … the Fed has resorted to a radical, uncharted spree of money printing. But the flood of liquidity, instead of spurring banks to lend and corporations to spend, has stayed trapped in the canyons of Wall Street, where it is inflating yet another unsustainable bubble. When it bursts, there will be no new round of bailouts like the ones the banks got in 2008. Instead, America will descend into an era of zero-sum austerity and virulent political conflict, extinguishing even today's feeble remnants of economic growth.*[21]

Therefore, should the question now be: are cyclical economic crises a common feature of market economies? Or are they a characteristic of Western "conventional" economies? China's development experience over the past more than 30 years has updated our fundamental understanding of how we perceive economic cycles.

5. How China Overcame Periodic Crises

The forces that led to the end of the boom and the beginning of the decline were twofold. One was on the supply side, whereby prosperity brought about the increase in production and investment costs. The other was on the demand side, whereby a relatively fast increase in incomes brought about a lower marginal propensity to consume. These two factors in combination effectively caused an overall lack of demand. China, however, has basically avoided any interruption to its economic boom in almost 20 years. Its secret has been to find a solution to these two downward cyclical forces.

---

[21] David A. Stockman, "Sundown in America," *The New York Times*, March 31, 2013. Available at: http://www.nytimes.com/2013/03/31/opinion/sunday/sundown-in-america.html?pagewanted=all&_r=0._Stockman is the former Republican representative for the state of Michigan and from 1981 to 1985 served as the director of the Office of Management and Budget in the administration of President Ronald Reagan. His most work includes "The Great Deformation: The Corruption of Capitalism in America" Public Affairs, 2013.

In fact, this is exactly what was done. From 1994 onwards, China has overcome the cyclical fluctuations that cause boom to turn to bust, greatly lengthening the cycle of prosperity and realizing sustained high growth. The reasons for this can be found by examining the two sides of supply and demand. On the supply side, the socialist market economic system produced by reforms was in place by the mid-1990s and had begun to operate normally. The system had the innate ability to curb rising costs during boom times while lifting the business sector's sustained investment interest and intensity, thus providing super strong investment drive. On the demand side, China was staunchly committed to further opening its markets — especially joining the World Trade Organization — and be fully integrated into the global economy. It also aimed to steadily increase the scale of international trade and the trade surplus. Because of this, it could use demand from the international market to effectively make up for the lack of domestic demand. From China's point of view, international purchasing power was external, so it could be called "third-party purchasing power" or "extraordinary buying power."

China has experienced more than 30 years of supernormal growth. This has been due, first, to the fact its unique market economic system can sustain a much stronger investment drive than conventional economies and therefore overcome short-term downturns with continued high investment. Second, the existence of the international market's supernormal purchasing power enabled China through a massive trade surplus to achieve the effective utilization of excess manufacturing capacity. Or we can say that China has successfully leveraged the international market's supernormal purchasing power by building a unique and strategic unconventional market economy and achieving sustained growth. Therefore, looking at China's annual average expansion of more than 10% since 1994, we can break it down into two parts: first, the normal growth rate of a conventional economy and second, a supplemental growth rate created by China's socialist market system.

The supplemental growth rate can probably be measured in two ways: the first is by looking at the trade surplus as a percentage of GDP. From 1978 to 2011, that ratio was 1.93% and between 1994 and 2011, it was 3.78%.[22] Second, we can look at India as a reference. In Table 1.2, India's economy from 1994 to 2011 saw average growth rise to 6.97% after the successful implementation of reform. China's economy grew by an average of 10.08% during the same period, about 3% higher, which was roughly the same as the ratio of China's trade surplus as part of GDP. Roughly speaking, the supernormal growth experienced over the more than 30 years since reform and opening included a supplemental growth rate of about 2%, with that rising to 3% after 1994.

Finally, China managed to break the cyclical forces seen in conventional economies and achieve supernormal growth. From the supply side, the special characteristics of its market economy produced exceptionally strong investment drive, while on the demand side, from the process of globalization emerged supernormal international purchasing power. The following chapter discuss how China's special market economy and the extraordinary international purchasing power were the two drivers of supernormal economic growth.

[22] National Statistics Bureau of China, "China Statistical Yearbook 2012," China Statistics Press, 2012.

Chapter 2

China's Special Market Economy and Supernormal Investment

As we have discussed, looking at it from the supply side, the basis for the nation's supernormal growth has been the socialist market economic system with Chinese characteristics, which the author has labeled as a "three-dimensional market structure."[1] We will explore more deeply the main themes of the three-dimensional system elsewhere. At this point, we will just explain how China's socialist market economy produced a mechanism for creating extraordinary investment forces from the perspective of economic growth.

[1] "Three-dimensional market system." This term was first used in May 2008 by this author while delivering an address titled "China's Reform as Indigenous Institutional Innovations" by invitation at Cornell University. This address was later titled "Unprecedented 30 Years: The Political Economy of China's Development Path" and included in the following book edited by the author. "Sanshinian yu Liushinian — Zhongguo de Gaige yu Fazhan [30 years and 60 years: China Reform and Development]", Truth and Wisdom Press, Shanghai People's Press, 2009.

1. Competitive Local Governments and the Three-dimensional Market System

The so-called three-dimensional market system is comparable to the conventional market economic structures in the West.[2] Simply put, in a conventional market system, there are two main parts: (i) government and (ii) private enterprise. The relationship between these two entities forms the main axle of the market economy. In China's existing system, besides the central government and competitive enterprise, there is one additional entity: the system of competitive local governments. This is illustrated in Figure 2.1.

Of course, many countries with market economies have local governments, but it is important to stress that the local governments in China are quite distinctive and different. Not only are they "governments," but they are also real economic entities. Local governments form a competitive economic structure and together with competitive enterprise make up the main body of the system, within which they share an almost equally important status and position.

Why is it that we describe local governments in China as innate economic microcosms within the economic system? There are four main reasons: first, motiving. Because of contract responsibility

---

[2] The main focus here is the similarities among the economic systems of Western countries. In actual fact, although they have the same market economies, the specific institutional arrangements — especially the relationship between government and enterprise, the system of income distribution, worker involvement in business management and the structure and operation of public finances — can exist in many quite different forms in advanced Western nations. From academia we can see that there are all types of divisions between market economies: Britain and America have the "Anglo-Saxon Model," Germany has the "Rhine Model," Northern Europe has the "Scandinavian models" and there is the "East Asian Model." For further research on this question, see David Coates, "Models of Capitalism: Growth and Stagnation in the Modern Era," Blackwell Publishers, 2001; Andrew Shonfield, "Modern Capitalism: The Changing Balance of Public and Private Power," Oxford University Press, 1965; Peter A. Hall and David Soskice, "Varieties of Capitalism: The Institutional Foundations of Comparative Advantage," Oxford University Press, 2001; Richard Whitley, "Business Systems in East Asia: Firms, Markets and Societies," SAGE Publications Ltd, 1994.

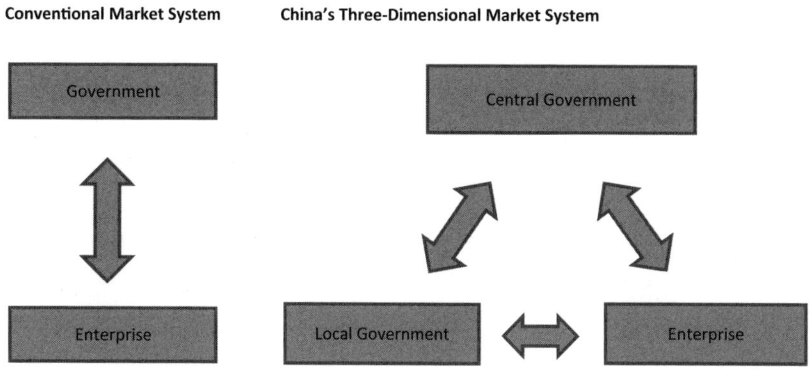

Figure 2.1 The Main Structures of the Two Types of Market Economic Systems.

system of finance and Tax Distribution System after 1994, local governments became sharers of the surplus value in their particular areas. And thus, local governments had strong motivation to promote local development; second, pressure. There was widespread competition among local governments, which caused pressure for advancement; third, authority and resources. As part of reform and opening up, the central government gave local authorities extensive powers in policy making and implementation. Additionally, state-owned assets, land value appreciation and local financing platforms gave the local governments the resources to promote economic development; fourth, the ability at management of local development. Like learning the art of war during wartime, the process of managing the local economy made authorities improve their handling and regulation of their economic power.

We will explore these points in more detail below.

(1) *The Tax distribution System and the Pursuit of Development*

Based on the experience of conventional market economies, the government's function in the process of modern economic growth is to exercise macroeconomic controls and formulate industrial policy. Local governments are just one layer of a national government system and do not have the authority to formulate macroeconomic policy. They mainly serve to implement the policies from the central authorities. Therefore, effect of local governments in a conventional market is not clear. Their main function is to provide regional public services. After reform and opening up, the role of local governments underwent a massive change. In the early years, contract responsibility system to a certain extent spurred the enthusiasm of local governments for developing their regional economies. The implementation of the tax sharing system in 1994 established a relatively stable mechanism under which tax revenue was allocated between central and local governments. With this reform, the tax revenue was divided into three portions: a fixed portion for the central government, a fixed portion for the local government and a third portion shared between both of them.[3] In this way, the local governments would have clearer expectations of how much income they can share in their jurisdiction during the process of development, leading to more stable economic behavior.

In the literature of economics, Karl Marx said that the pursuit of surplus value was the perpetual economic motivating force for capitalists. In the theory of New Institutional Economics, people used residual claim rights to describe the same phenomenon.[4] Now, local governments,

[3] For further reading on financial reform and the tax sharing system, see "Zhongguo Sanshinian Caishui Gaige de Huigu yu Zhanwang [China Taxation Reform in the last 30 Years: Retrospective and Prospects]" as published in "Zhongguo Jingji 50ren Kan Sanshinian — Huigu yu Fenxi [Chinese Economists 50 Forum Looking at Thirty Years: Retrospective and Analysis]," ed. Wu Jinglian, China Economy Publishing House, 2008; Xu Shanda, Wosuo Jingli de Caishuigage de Huiyi Pianduan [My Fragmented Recollections of Taxation Reform] as published in "Zhongguo Jingji Wushiren Kan Sanshinian — Huigu yu Fenxi [Chinese Economists 50 Forum Looking at Thirty Years: Retrospective and Analysis]", ed. Wu Jinglian, China Economy Publishing House, 2008; For analysis of theories on taxation reform, see Yang Zhiyong and Yang Zhigang, "Zhongguo Caizheng Zhidu Gaige Sanshinian [China's 30 Years of Taxation Reform]", Trut and Freedom Press, Shanghai People's Press, 2008.

[4] Regarding "surplus value," in Karl Marx's original concept (1867), he accuses capitalists of appropriating the excess value from workers; "residual claimant" was the idea of property rights economics (Harold Demsetz and Armen Alchian, 1972) and ownership was only related to the breakdown of the results of business operations. The difference in their wording reflects the differences in their standpoints. But as one of

enterprises and the central government all take a certain share of all income from within the jurisdiction of local authorities after costs have been deducted. In this way, local governments became a constant sharer of the surplus value in their regions, and thus became an economic entity who possesses the right to share in stable profits of enterprises. Professor Steven N. S. Cheung describes this not as "taxation" but instead, in the economic sense, as "rent."[5] Thus, as enterprises generally pursue market share and profits, local governments have come from within the system to provide strong and sustained growth momentum.

(2) *The Pressure of Competition*

The common to view Chinese government as a centralized organization in which officials are appointed by the senior leadership, lower ranks are subordinate to the senior cadres and the government bureaucratic system is a relationship between those who lead and those who are led. But China's government system is massive. From a vertical perspective, it is a hierarchical relationship; from a horizontal view, it is a parallel relationship. During the period of reform and opening up, the central government used a decentralized assessment management system and put both motivity and pressure to local government. Provincial-level authorities also used similar policies with the governments of local areas and cities under their jurisdiction to encourage competition among them. Additionally, on the macro level, the central government attaches overriding importance

---

the elements of product value, they are the same thing. Professor Yu Guangyuan (1979) recommended using the term "residual value" to refer to a socialist economy to explain this question. For more on the modern development of Marx's value theory, see Shi Zhengfu, "Xiandai Qiyezhong de Laodong yu Jiazhi: Makesi Jiazhililun de Xiandai Tuozhan [Labor and Value in Modern Firms: A Modern Extension of Marx's Value Theory]", Shanghai People's Press, 2002.

[5] See Steven N. S. Cheung, "Zhongguo de Jingji Zhidu [The Economic System of China]", China CITIC Arcadia Press, 2009. Professor Cheung's dissertation that one part of the Chinese government's income is "rent" and not "tax" is a revolutionary idea in re-evaluating the government's properties as part of the socialist market economy. But it has not yet garnered enough attention.

to promoting economic development, using this as an important basis for assessment. The result is that local governments are all equal competitors regardless of their ranking. A county-level government could compete with a city-level authority outside the province or even directly with the authority of another province.

This distinguishing feature was created after reform and opening up.

Today, looking at the Chinese government from a horizontal perspective, 2,000 to 3,000 county-level governments and several hundred prefecture and city governments all seek economic development within their jurisdictions, causing competition among them to become commonplace. For example, Kunshan in Jiangsu Province. Against the background of reform and opening up, this county-level unit recorded such rapid growth that the scale of its economy exceeded many prefecture-level municipalities, even approaching the economies of some sub-provincial cities.[6] One of the main reasons for this was its advantage of being in geographical proximity to Shanghai. This enabled it to take a more vigorous approach toward attracting investment. With higher quality services, it competed directly with Shanghai, leading many foreign companies that had been planning to establish themselves in China's main

[6]The following statistics are based on data published in the "2011 Kunshan City National Economic and Social Development Statistics Report" compiled by the city's statistics bureau: in 2011, Kunshan's GDP reached RMB243.225 billion, forming a single RMB100 billion industry cluster and 11 RMB10 billion industry clusters. Among these was the RMB100 billion IT cluster (including telecommunication equipment, motherboard makers and other electronics equipment) which saw output reach RMB451.26 billion; for the whole year 8,119 new domestic enterprises were added with registered capital of RMB24.947 billion; 387 new foreign ventures were approved with registered foreign capital of US$3.246 billion. The Taiwan Electrical and Electronic Manufacturers' Association annual survey of the investment environment in Mainland China ranked Kunshan as the best city for three years in a row in terms of its overall economic strength; Forbes rated Kunshan as the best county-level city in China for three years in a row and for the past seven years has been included in the list of top small and medium-sized cities in terms of scientific development. As a county-level city of two million people, Kunshan's 2011 GDP exceeded that of Naning, Taiyuan, Urumqi and Zhuhai.

commercial city, to end up investing in Kunshan instead. This resulted in it becoming the world's largest manufacturing base for the information technology industry. For a county-level city to compete directly with a provincial-level municipality is enough to show that the competition between local governments is real and profound. The facts show that while the form and method of competition are different compared with that among enterprises, the depth and intensity are in no way inferior.[7]

(3) *The Local Governments' Authority and Resources to Promote Development of their Areas*

Apart from general fiscal revenue, Chinese regional government also have resources, something their counterparts in Western countries do not. First, after 1949, China gradually accumulated the assets of state-owned enterprises.[8] The enterprises along the coast had reached a considerable scale even before reform and opening up. In line with the deepening market reforms and especially after 15 years of sustained economic expansion, they had shown impressive development. The value of the state-owned enterprises under the control of the local governments multiplied correspondingly. An example is state-owned distilleries and breweries, which have

---

[7]Why is there so much fierce competition like this among local governments? Professor Steven N. S. Cheung wrote "Zhongguo de Jingji Zhidu [The Economic System of China]" (China CITIC Arcadia Press, 2009) to mark 30 years of reform and in it he explained the economics of the competition using the concept of "rent." In the opinion of this author, this book has groundbreaking significance in its theories on the emerging political and economic system with Chinese characteristics. On the same topic, there are also other theories. For example, Professors Xu Chenggang and Qian Yingyi's (1993), "The Theory of the M-form Structure," Zhou Lian's (2007, 2008), "Political Tournament Model"; Zhang Jun and Zhou Lian, "Weizengzhang er Jingzheng: Zhongguo Zengzhang de Zhengzhijingjixue", Truth and Wisdom Press, Shanghai People's Press, 2008. This book is a collection of some of major articles regarding this issue.

[8]Data based on the Ministry of Finance of the People's Republic of China's "Accounting Yearbook of China 2011." The total asset of state-owned companies in 2010 was RMB64.02143 trillion.

operations in many areas. Their values went from the tens of millions of RMB to the hundreds of millions and then into the billions, like the producers of maotai liquor, whose market capitalizations are measured in the hundreds of billions.[9] Other examples include real estate companies, city investment firms and especially solar power and photovoltaic companies, many Local governments realized several dozen times earning by investing in these companies. Second, land development led to land financing, which constituted another major asset for local governments. Because of public ownership, the process of converting land from agriculture usage into industrial, commercial and residential applications itself had a massive one-off appreciation. This change in classification caused an increase in the land's price and had little relationship to how it was being managed by the persons involved and could be called an incremental appreciation of the original land value. In line with general economic wisdom regarding land values, as a country's level of industrialization, urbanization and gentrification increases, the incremental increase in land values become larger.

Against a backdrop of 15 years of fast-paced urbanization and industrialization in the last 15 years, the scale of the incremental increase in land values has risen by leaps and bounds. By managing the development of primary land, local governments created favorable material conditions for attracting investment and also accumulated vast sums of money for local public finance. Upon state-owned assets and land finance, local government's financing platform evolved. Thus, local governments gradually came to resemble investment firms and became economic entities that operated capital. At the same time, they accumulated more and more experience from practice.

[9] Data compiled from Shanghai Stock Exchange statements. Kweichow Moutai Co., Ltd. (600519). Using the company's closing share price on the day of listing in 2001 of RMB35.55, the company's market capitalization was RMB6.2 billion. About 10 years later it broke through RMB200 billion.

Currently, more and more local governments are beginning to use various types of modern financial tools including banks, investment trusts, equity investments, funds and public listings to manage their assets and liabilities. In terms of autonomy of local development, opposite to general view of highly centralized system, local governments actually had room for policy making, feedback and implementation, since central government tended to make policy general and abstract. In China, because management of personnel, finances and administration are still in the early stages of development, the autonomy of local governments in making decisions regarding revenue, budget setting and implementation and the selection and appointment of officials is far greater than can be imagined. This autonomy affords the governments a great deal of leeway in their policy-making efficiency and effectiveness of implementation with regards to developing their local areas.

(4) *The Ability at Management of Local Development*

Today, the media pays more attention to corruption and bureaucracy among government officials, and the public image of officials is often related with empty talk and boring speech. This has led most people to seriously underestimate the abilities of local government officials in China, but in fact, their ability is superb.

Competition is the greatest motivator for learning. Because of the existence of horizontal competition discussed above, "learning by doing" becomes the only way for officials to improve themselves and local governments become "big schools" for officials to promote their ability. Most government officials today have formal higher education backgrounds. Additionally, the process of taking up a post must be done step-by-step, with experience first gained in different positions and through all grades of training. In the process of promotion, officials must receive training at party schools and formal institutions, which can even include advanced studies at internationally-renowned universities. Even more importantly, local government officials are now facing challenges that defy the imagination. Even though they are constrained by all types of regulations and laws under the government system and are not as free as their corporate counterparts, local officials on many occasions must confront all types of challenges, just like executives in the corporate sector. They must contend also with political study and handling emergencies, while also dealing with conventional business negotiations.

Attracting investment by its nature is a special type of business activity. Local government's finance platform essentially has characteristic of modern finance. When this type of new economic phenomenon first began appearing, people did not really understand much about it and easily made mistakes. But with accumulated experience, local officials achieved progress. In their handling of reorganizing companies after bankruptcy, planning area development, directing large-scale projects, managing resources, project appraisals and personnel management, we could say that the practise of officials now has surpassed the scope of anything contained in business textbooks or current economic theory. This accumulation of experience is a very valuable factor for China. It is a treasure trove within which is condensed developmental knowledge and talent. Only by relying on the contingent of government officials who improved constantly, China's local governments could take advantage of reform and opening up under the push of internal competition and eternal pressure, and finally became a significant force to the nation's economic growth.

In summary, China's local governments have dual identities. One is the bureaucratic hierarchy within the system of government, fulfilling its functions of administering society, embodying its role as public affairs manager. The other reflects its role as a manager of a region's development using its internal drive and resources for planning, investment in new ventures, supporting enterprises and promoting economic growth. In this second role, the competitive system made up of local governments and that of enterprises are both interdependent and mutually independent. This encapsulates the special market economy produced by the competitive nature of the local government system, namely the "three-dimensional market economy."

The functions of administering public affairs and managing local development constitute the two main missions of local governments. To adapt to a broadening of these functions, their organizational structure must also undergo changes accordingly. There must be the formation of two departments whose division of labor is clearly defined, with one purely handling public affairs and the other economic management. Apart from departments managing government administration, public security and judicial matters, culture, education, public health and other public affairs, the local government also has a large number of organizations and personnel that may or may not be on formal contracts. Their entire responsibility is in the service of economic development. Often, this part of local governments resemble companies in their organization and their overriding task is to attract more capital, technology and companies to their region, boosting GDP, employment and tax revenue. This is a Chinese phenomenon and a special characteristic of the nation.

2. Local Investment Incentives and Levels of Investment

The economic activities of local governments naturally led to changes in certain practices and interactions within the business system and the rules of market operations. Compared with conventional market economies, the operation of China's three-dimensional market system had many new, special characteristics. We will briefly explain its impaction investment levels.

(1) *Higher-Than-Normal Investment Rates*

Investment incentives offered by local governments caused the scale of investment by Chinese enterprises to be significantly larger than the amount invested by companies in conventional market economies. To promote development, apart from investing in basic local infrastructure, the government also provides a whole package of incentives for business ventures. For example, preferential land prices. Under a unified government land price-setting system, the government can attract businesses by offering land at below market rates, which could be in the form of land abatements, future tax offsets or the use of tax rebate to tangibly reduce land costs for companies. For companies of special importance, these types of preferential packages could go as far as offering land for free or even at negative values. For the acquisition of equipment and technology, the government can offer direct financial subsidies. If companies that are investing in the area badly need to import advanced technologies or require advanced manufacturing equipment whose investment value is relatively large, the government can offer direct subsidies to encourage the use of new technologies and equipment. The classic example is the light emitting diode (LED) and semiconductor chip companies, whereby all regions use a single-device subsidy system.

Apart from the above incentives, local governments will also offer supplementary equity investments or financing assistance. For high-tech companies that have good prospects, but are lack of funds, local governments will often take the initiative to assist firms in arranging financing. Sometimes, it will serve as a "subordinated beneficiary" to directly take an equity stake in the company, showing an willing to burden most of the risk in order to attract investor. Also, when a company is on its initial stage of founding and high risk period, local government would invest in the first place, and when the company grows mature, local government tends to transfer its shareholdings and exist the investment. The accrued funds from this venture can be used to invest in the next small-to-middle-sized company.

Apart from the efforts above, local governments also offer assistance in coordinating and organizing recruitment, especially when attracting high-level talents, local governments employ a comprehensive set of measures to attract high-level talent. They also provide policy supports, help enterprises contact with banks and get loans, and even assist enterprises in organizing key materials, expanding markets and handling economic disputes. All of these actions lower the investment costs of enterprises.

Of course, different enterprises receive different types of assistance, which is determined by various factors such as the region's current economic conditions, local government's demand of investment, enterprise's position in its area and the externality enterprise would bring about. By examining some of the cases, we find that the percentage of the incentive investment from local government in company's total investment differs very much. The portion can be as low as 10% up to as much as 20–30%. Individual enterprises can even get most of the funds for their initial investment from the governments.

To sum up, a considerable portion of the investment costs in Chinese start-up ventures are given as incentives by local governments, which means that they are markedly lower than those facing companies in conventional market economies. And in line with basic economic common sense, the scale of a company's investment is dependent on the returns and costs. In the case where investment returns are a given and costs fall, the scale of the investment will increase.

Figure 2.2 describes the above scenario. Figure 2.2a shows the scale of investment under a conventional economy, with MC1 representing the marginal cost of investment and the downward sloping curve representing the level of marginal return on investment. Both lines intersect at *E*1, with the scale of investment corresponding to the horizontal axis at *I*1. Figure 2.2b shows the scale of investment under China's market economic system. Because investment costs of enterprises in China are lower than those for their counterparts in conventional economies, we will drop the position of the marginal cost curve from MC1 to MC2. As the graph shows, because the MCI is lowered, it causes the marginal return on investment axis to move downward and to the right from E_1 to E_2. Correspondingly, the scale of investment also increases from I_1 to I_2.

This indicates that with local government incentives, the investment costs are lowered for businesses and the scale of the investments are increased, which is reflected in the macroeconomic system by higher investment rates in the national economy. Thus, we can confirm that since reform and opening up the Chinese economy has

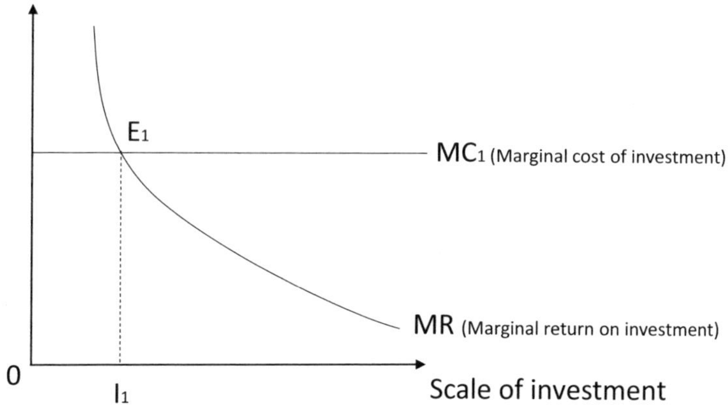

Figure 2.2a Rate of Investment in a Conventional Economy.

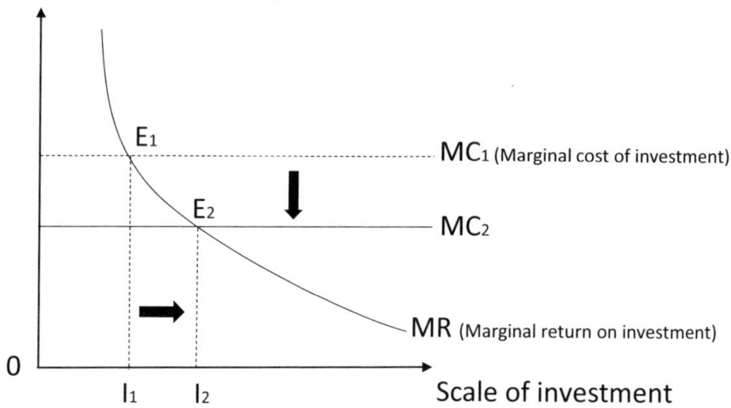

Figure 2.2b Rate of Investment in China's Market Economic System.

maintained high investment rates, part of which is due to the relatively high savings rate and the other is the innate system of local government incentives.

It must be pointed out that government incentives often have a counter-cyclical effect. Under normal conditions, offering economic incentives to attract investment and appeal to companies to set up business in their areas is routine work. But when the macroeconomic environment is experiencing a downturn, and especially when external factors cause a decline, local governments empathize with the companies struggling to survive out of consideration of maintaining their area's economic development. They are even more motivated to resolve the economic issues. Because China's economic system is very integrated, as soon as it starts to experience crisis, all levels of government from the central authorities to regional leadership implement appropriate policy incentives. Thus, at these times, local governments generally increase their support efforts. And as they have a relatively large amount of autonomy, different governments can tailor their rescue plans to especially suit the conditions in their own areas.

Often at these times of difficulty, governments will pay close attention to each other's plight and learn from the other's experience. For example, in 2007 as the US subprime mortgage was engulfing the world causing the global economy to slow, all kinds of relief measures and policies were implemented across China. One well-known case was in Zhejiang Province, where the government set a precedent in regards to participating in a special loan project, leading banks to offer the large majority of a loan package to assist selected businesses. The governments vowed that if these loan packages caused any debt crises, it would use its own funds to assume the risk of bad loans. This prompted the banking system to broaden their support for distressed businesses. Some areas also implemented tax cuts and related support measures for struggling enterprises, while others used their channel advantages to help companies promote products or allocate resources. In short, the related policies and measures promulgated one after the other by every level of local government meant that their investment incentives had the special characteristic of countering the effects of cyclical volatility.

(2) *Comparatively Low Transaction Fees*

Local governments offer a comprehensive range of support services to help Chinese companies within their jurisdiction lower their transaction costs and, consequently, boost the region's development.

It is similar to how the corporate headquarters of a major company in the West might offer assistance to its subsidiaries. From observing this experience, the support services offered by governments have helped lower the general transaction costs for company operations. Nobel laureates Ronald Harry Coase and Oliver E. Williamson introduced the concept of transaction costs, which became a field in modern economics that developed very rapidly.[10] So-called transaction costs are the related fees for everything that goes into the process of successfully completing a business transaction, such as contract drafting, negotiations, contract signing and execution. Because all sides of a business transaction are looking to maximize their own interests in a kind of opportunism amid an environment of uncertainty, there exists a great amount of risk in any contract, right from the negotiation stage to execution, the costs of which should not be underestimated. In actual fact, according to estimates from scholars of new institutional economics, transaction costs in the US economy account for a high proportion of the national income and this trend is clearly continuing to rise.[11] Consider for a moment the huge scale of the legal profession in the US as well as the business of auditing, public relations, consulting and ratings agencies. The transaction costs in the modern market economy are evidently massive.

[10] Ronald H. Coase, "The Nature of the Firm," *Economica*, 1937, Vol. 4, No. 16: 386–405. The Chinese edition: "Qiye de Xingzhi" reprinted from "Qiye, Shichang yu Falu," Trans. Sheng Hong, Chen Yu, Truth and Wisdom Press, SJPC, Shanghai People's Press, 2009; Oliver E. Williamson, "The Economic Institutions of Capitalism," New York: Free Press, 1985. Chinese edition: "Zibenzhuyi Jingji Zhidu — Lun Qiye Qianyue yu Shichang Qianyue," Trans. Duan Yicai, Wang Wei, Commercial Press, 2009.

[11] For reference, see J. Wallis and D. North, "Measuring the Transaction Sector in the American Economy, 1870–1970," in S. Engerman and R. Gallman (eds.), "Long-term Factors in American Economic Growth", Chicago: University of Chicago Press, 1986, pp. 95–161; Erik G. Furubotn and Rudolf Richter, "Xinzhidu Jingjixue: Yige Jiaoyi Feiyong Fenxi Fanshi [Institutions and Economic Theory: The Contribution of the New Institutional Economics]," Trans. Jiang Jianqiang and Luo Changyuan, SJPC, Shanghai People's Press, 2006.

In US economics, transaction costs are often applied to analyze the costs incurred when companies are doing business. But in the process of doing business, companies do not just need to deal with other companies, they also have to engage with all types of non-business entities such as communities, residents, labor and regulators. We can classify transaction costs into two categories: the first type is those arising from transactions with other businesses and the second type is those from transactions with non-businesses. Experience has shown that Chinese local governments often serve as the internal facilitator in the process of conducting "type two" transactions, adopting many different roles. When a company's project requires land, it will not rely on lawyers to bargain with all the landowners one after the other as their counterparts in Western countries must do. Instead, they look to the government, which often will first expropriate the land from farmers, connect all utilities, services and roads and then hand it over to the business. When businesses do not have the funds for construction, the government may offer an abatement on the purchase with the funds gradually repaid once the company begins operations and is generating profits.

In the initial stages after a company is established, it may not have sufficient credit history to apply for a loan with a bank and, again, often the government will come forward and coordinate between the business and the banks to recommend the enterprise. It also could arrange surety for the loan to facilitate securing of the funds. And if businesses are to develop, they need to upgrade their employees. Governments can use the advantages of its organizational structure and channels to assist in recruitment, providing reduced taxes on personal income, housing subsidies, child schooling and other incentives to attract talent.

When companies encounter misfortune — for example, if technology is stolen or funds defrauded — companies often cannot wait for the outcome of protracted legal proceedings involved with litigation. Instead, frequently it is the government that will intervene using the law enforcement and judicial means at its disposal to swiftly resolve the matter. If an enterprise encounters labor disputes, often they do not only pursue legal action, it is likely that the relevant government department will also step in and participate in reconciliation. In all areas of a company's functional management, from administration, personnel, financing and legal affairs to product development and marketing, local governments often are a significant participant. In a sense, they make up half of the management team at the corporate headquarters of companies within their area of jurisdiction. On this point, Professor Steven N. S. Cheung offers a vivid description:

> *Require a business license? The county government will send someone to do the running about for you. Need a building permit? The government will guarantee it. You don't like that dirty little creek that runs past your land? They might dam it up into a little lake for you. They will help you find an architect, a builder and when you're preparing to start operations, they'll help you hire staff for a reasonable fee. Yes, counties have teams to recruit workers and do the hiring for the investors. They will promote their cheap power rates to you, their parks and entertainment, their convenient transportation, the supply of their utilities, their glorious history and even the beauty of their women — I am not exaggerating!*[12]

To sum up, with all other external factors being equal, all the different types of "management services" provided by the local authorities mean a huge reduction in the "type two" transaction costs for company operations. In a conventional two-dimensional economy, the transaction contracts between businesses and non-businesses usually have to go through intermediary services like lawyers, auditors, consultants and political lobbyists before they can be completed. While this method may appear more formal and fair, it is time-consuming, inefficient and the fees are high. Additionally, in China when a local government steps in to assist market entities by offering a framework for negotiations or resolution of disputes or even arbitration, while it may not necessarily be fair, it can resolve special problems that arise between companies and non-companies

---

[12] Steven N. S. Cheung, "Zhongguo de Jingji Zhidu [The Economic System of China]," China CITIC Arcadia Press, 2009.

over contracts more effectively than if the business tried handling the matter by themselves. Thus, it is highly efficient and lowers the overall cost to the rest of society.

(3) *Higher Administrative Efficiency*

In China's three-dimensional market system, because of the intervention of local governments, the existence of departmental bureaucracy, which is common among modern governments, is to a certain extent balanced out and resolved, greatly facilitating a company's operations. So-called departmental bureaucracy is intended to refer to the natural tendency of certain government departments to work strictly in accordance with the rules, dragging their feet, these kinds of inefficient practices. When they get involved in resource allocation, it results in corrupt practices like manipulation, nest feathering and fraud. The reason for this can be traced to the fact that these departments are not independent bodies and they do not have any hard performance constraints. It is difficult to use any economic indicators to evaluate individuals in office and instead most are appraised by using internal qualitative assessments, so there is no intrinsic motivation to pursue self-development and opportunities. And because there is a monopoly on power in the external environment, there is no pressure from market competition.

This kind of departmental bureaucracy, which in modern economic theory is called the "principal agent problem," is common and unavoidable in any kind of formal organization whether it be in government, large corporations, universities and church groups.[13]

[13] Bureaucracy has the same meaning as hierarchy and both terms are often used interchangeably. Explaining their meaning in traditional Western economics, bureaucracy and hierarchy originally were very neutral words. They were used to describe the dominant positions in all kinds of large organizations in modern society. For example, in the military, universities, business and politics. The well-known sociologist Max Weber (1978) created the modern theories of bureaucracy, which were later developed and improved by France's Michael Crozier among other scholars. Today at universities in the US, there are subject categories called "organizational sociology" and at schools of management, there are studies in

Starting from the rationalization of procedures and budgeting in modern public administration, attempts to resolve the chronic problem of departmental bureaucracy, while achieving some success, ultimately failed. They also were unable to touch the authority of government departments or develop any impetus or competitive pressure to address these core problems. In a great number of developing countries, because of complex historical issues and social infrastructure, the development of bureaucracy will serve a criminally bad government.

The reform of the Chinese government has taken a different path. As mentioned above, decentralization, the giving of concessions and empowerment are all essentially to offer room in which local governments can develop. This affords internal drive and external competition and thereby transforming the official or "agent" into an alternative type of business executive or "principal." The result is in the process of balancing and suppressing the traditional departmental bureaucracy, the local governments become a key player: as they are opposed to the central government's reliance on departmental bureaucracy and the business community must get approval from the multitude of layers within the system, they become partners in getting the job done.

It should be pointed out that the existence of so many government departments is a necessary condition for the normal operation of society and the economy. For example, environmental protection, food safety, workplace safety, fire and emergency services, business registration, business statistics, tax collection, legislative regulation and law enforcement. No country is exempt from having government handling these matters. The context in China also includes the two

---

"organizational design." A classic text on the subject is Michael Crozier "The Bureaucratic Phenomenon," Chicago: University of Chicago Press, 1964. Chinese edition: "Keceng Xianxiang," Trans. Liu Hanquan, Shanghai People's Press, 2002; W. A. Niskanen Jr., "Bureaucracy and Representative Government," Chicago: Aldine Atherton, 1971; W. A. Niskanen Jr., "Bureaucrats and Politicians," *Journal of Law and Economics*, December, 1975, 18, pp. 617–643; Gordon Tullock, "The Politics of Bureaucracy," Washington DC: Public Affairs Press, 1965.

important items of state resource management and industry regulation. Imagine if a single company wanted to make an investment for development, to get the project initiated it had to get the verification, approval and coordination from so many government departments. Even if it was done in accordance with the rule of law in a country where such as system is relatively strong, like in European nations or America, the level of administrative efficiency would still often result in protracted delays.

In fact, in the US and the developed countries of Europe today, often years and decades are wasted before work on the slightly more complex large-scale projects can begin, which precisely illustrates their administrative inefficiency. Consider the long shadow of China's more than 2,000-year history of centralized government bureaucracy and it is reasonable to say that today the extent of this problem ought to have far surpassed that of the developed nations of Europe and America. But in actual fact, the administrative efficiency of China's government is significantly higher than in those countries. A normal industrial project basically can be approved within a year. Even major projects that require approval of the National Development and Reform Commission like car factories or large-scale chemical plants and major infrastructure projects rarely take more than three-to-five years. Every year in China, it is generally acknowledged that projects that are started and completed are too many to easily count and include power stations, ports, roads, railway lines, hospitals, schools, parks, theatres, libraries and museums among others.

It should be said that local governments play a key role in this process. Fundamentally speaking, in the process of negotiating the labyrinths of departmental bureaucracy, the local governments and enterprises become comrades in arms in the trenches. And as local government leaders and departmental officials are part of the same government system, throughout the course of their careers with changes in jobs and promotions, both groups often work together and cooperate or swap roles. In this way, each becomes familiar with the other's work processes and habits enabling them to communicate more easily.

Furthermore, the purpose of "blending together" local government leadership and department officials was to assist companies within their jurisdictional districts and promote the region's development. This is consistent with the major goal of national advancement and thus clearly has a higher level of influence and credibility. It is interesting that while local governments also have their own layered bureaucracy with departments, commissions, offices and bureaus, the gap between them and the leadership is narrow, making them easier to control. Additionally, when dealing with bureaucratic superiors, they again became part of the leadership's working mechanism.

In this way, it often becomes a strategic game between the local bureaucratic departments and businesses led by the local governments and the higher-ranking bureaucratic departments. The result was that China's three-dimensional market system largely resolved the problem of departmental bureaucracies and low administrative efficiency that commonly exists in other countries around the world.

Of course, bureaucracy in government is still a widespread and serious problem today in China. Mainly, it is a process of formulating regulations by the national-level professional ministries that are too closed and simple, with many processes a vague blur and no clear or workable checks on how cases are accepted and resolved. What is more, a situation whereby "national authority is undermined by departmental one, and departmental authority is undermined by individual one" still exists to a certain extent, which impairs the effectiveness of the government and lowers its reputation and authority. But with this kind of departmental bureaucracy, even as it is a common failing among nations with modern governments, it is China's history that carries the heaviest burden. In the three-dimensional market system, the institutionalization of the relatively autonomous rise to power of local governments was not only the cause of the above-mentioned problem, but in fact was the "Chinese antidote" in dealing with departmental bureaucracy.

To sum up, in comparing enterprises operating within China's three-dimensional market system and those in a conventional market system, it is clear that the former obviously have stronger motivation to invest, the speed with which departments handle project approval is much faster and the cost of handling all kinds of transactions with non-businesses is often lower. These factors combined enabled enterprises in China to form a kind of superior investment capability that surpasses private companies operating in conventional market economies. It is because this super investment ability is widespread that makes "market overheating" a special and regular characteristic of China's macroeconomy. But not in the same way as in a regular market economy, where there is always the worry of "insufficient effective demand."

3. Long-term Returns of Local Investment Incentives

Can the financial support provided to new ventures and the integrated services offered to companies by local governments be sustained? Evidently, this depends on the effectiveness of the fiscal and service support offered by the local governments. The subsidies and supporting services offered by local governments are actually a kind of investment behavior as they have a right to share the profits once the venture has successfully established itself. For shareholders, the future returns of the company are simple — the profits. To use the terminology of political economy, they are "residual value" or "residual claims." In contrast, through the provision of support to start-up ventures, the local governments have secured not only a "residual value" claim, but also a right to share the entire incomes and returns from these companies as well as their related industrial chains.

Firstly, Value-Added Taxes

Under the current tax law, regardless of whether a company makes any profits, if it has a factory that is in operation and generating income from sales, they must pay a 17% product value-added tax. Of that, the local government is entitled to 25%, or 4.25% points of the product value-added tax. Assuming the value-added of the products in terms of their overall value (in terms of sales) is 20–50%, this 4.25% is equal to about 0.85–2.125% of sales. In the electronics, household appliance and motor vehicle industries, the profit margin of many Chinese companies often does not exceed 5% and sometimes are only about 2%. That is, the local government's right to share in the returns of these companies in terms of value-added taxes has caught up with the entire amount of returns entitled to shareholders.

Secondly, Corporate Income Tax

Once a company starts to earn a profit and, excluding any agreements for tax breaks during the financial year, local governments can receive additional revenue through corporate income tax. Apart from high-tech companies, which are taxed at a rate of 15%, other normal enterprises must pay a 25% tax on profits. Previously, the contribution of this tax revenue to local governments was not as good as value-added taxation. But after a company upgrades its manufacturing operations and increases its scale, profit margins consequently increase and the contribution from corporate income tax rises. Given that corporate profits account for about 8% of revenue, the 25% taxation on earnings would be equal to about a 2% tax on revenue. So in terms of the local government, under most scenarios where sales profit margins reached 8%, it meant that the local share of corporate income tax and value-added taxes were basically the same.

Thirdly, Income Tax and Social Security on Employees

In providing salaries and bonuses to employees, companies must pay the tax on their income and the different types of social security contributions. Regardless of whether the company is making a profit, salaries are fixed in advance. If a company exists, then there are salaries and employee income tax to be paid and the enterprise, in accordance with regulations, must withhold the tax and pay it as well as the social security contributions. And when the employees take their salaries and spend it in daily life, they will incur yet another levy: consumption tax.

Fourthly, Related Business

There are also the related businesses spurred on around the company's operations. For example, the company's use of intermediary products such as components and raw materials. Once the company grows, its demand will grow, causing the agglomeration of intermediary suppliers and development of related local industries and trade. The scale of this economic activity and the increase in population will also drive development of the local business services industry and a boom in the property market.

This point has special relevance to local government finances. For local government land financing, the core issue is the breakdown of the ratio allotted to industrial, commercial and public use. It depends to a large extent on the money the government earns from commercial land as to whether it can hedge the losses it incurs on land for industrial use (due to its offering subsidies to businesses) and the costs of public land (public land earns no income). That amount of money depends on the price of the land, which is determined by the area's overall economic growth. Thus, related industries, population growth and the expansion of the total economy causes the real estate market to thrive, which has special significance to local government finances.

In summing up, the system of local government investment incentives has a chain-reaction effect on the region's development (see Figure 2.3).

From this, you can see that the local government's investment incentive policies are essentially a kind of investment behavior: it is a comprehensive, long-term investment for a share of a company's future profits and related returns. That is, the financial expenditures of the governments on these incentive systems have a different meaning to the normal public expenditures in the West, where they are generally just purely consumption expenditure: once the funds have been appropriated and spent, it is over. In contrast, the expenditures on investment incentives in China result in an unending expansion of value creation and a process of sharing, which ultimately increases tax revenue, share and land values and a whole host of other ways in which it finds its way back to the government's finances.

The relevance of this is that the government's outlay for the incentives is based on expectations of future returns, which is the

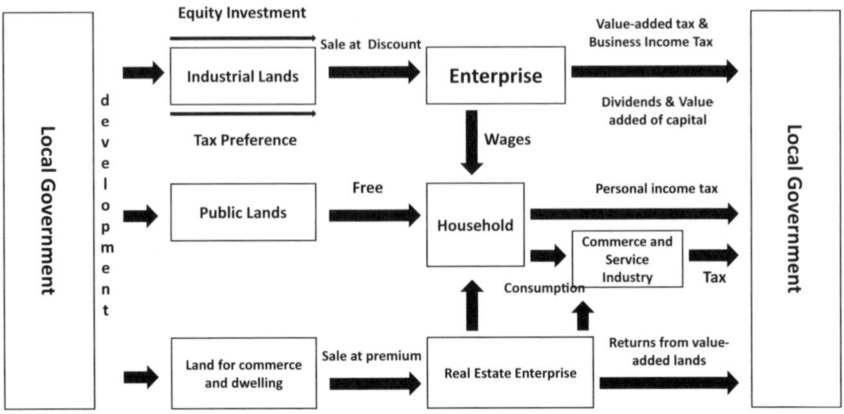

Figure 2.3 The Chain-Reaction Effect of Local Government Investment Incentives.

action of an investor. And these expectations inevitably result in motivation to seek a growth in returns. Logically, we can deduce that in the wake of local development and accumulation of practical experience, the local governments will improve their methods of investment incentives in order to secure as much future profit as possible. As this is realized, we can observe the large number of phenomena listed below: more and more governments directly link the extent of the incentives with the scale of the company's investment and even the future taxes paid as indicators; they increasingly focus on the area's resource advantages in selecting key industries; and the more advanced an area becomes, the more stress will be laid on selecting investments to attracting investments.

Since government finances are being used to invest in future returns, inevitably, it will result in going into debt to finance investments, which will in turn cause the emergence of a local financing platform. Investment and financing, assets and liabilities, will organically become an integral part of local government finance management. The problem does not lie in whether or not there are liabilities, but rather how those liabilities are utilized. Not the absolute size of the liability, but the relationship between the liability and the asset, namely the asset–liability ratio.[14] While the history of local government's managing their assets and liabilities is not long, it is gradually improving. From a long-term perspective, it is just a matter of maintaining competition, which with continued learning about the mechanisms supplemented with assistance and guidance from the central government and academia, China's special system of local government financial management will mature.

[14] Currently, Chinese academia commonly link government debt and national income, mainly when discussing the national debt to GDP ratio. This author believes the corresponding data set for government debt should be the state's net assets, not GDP. If we want to emphasize the ability to repay the debt, cash flow and related indicators should be used, such as debt payable annually and not the total liabilities. The annual free cash flow available for paying back debt is not national income or fiscal revenue. The mismatch about the concept of assets indicates academia is only in the initial stages of understanding the system of national assets and liabilities. Thankfully, more and more scholars are beginning to promote this area of study. See Li Yang, "Zhongguo Zhuquan Zichan Fuzhaibiao Ji Qifengxian Pinggubiao Yanjiu (I and II) [Chinese Sovereign Balance Sheet and Its Risk Assessment (I and II)]," *Economic Research Journal*, 2012. Vols. 6 and 7; Ma Jun, Zhang Xiaorong and Li Zhiguo, "Zhongguo Guojia Zichan Fuzhaibiao Yanjiu [A Study of China's National Balance Sheet]," Social Sciences Academic Press (China), 2012; Shen Peilong and Fan Huan, "Jiben Keliudongxing Zichan Fuzhaibiao de Woguo Zhengfu Zhaiwu Fengxian Yanjiu [A Study of the Chinese Government's Debt Risk Based on the Liquid Assets Balance Sheet]," *Economic Research Journal*, 2012, Vol. 2; Wu You, "Guomin Zichan Fuzhai Hesuan yu Kuaiji Zichan Fuzhai Hesuan de bijiao yu Zhuanhuan," Statistical Research, 2002, Vol. 4.

Chapter 3

The US Federal Reserve and International Supernormal Purchasing Power

Chapter 2 explained how that in China's special market economy, there exists a sustained, strong impetus for mega investment. But the problem of economic cycles cannot be solved by solely relying on this. As the period of sustained mega investment increases, the accumulation of new production capacity grows ever larger and the oversupply of consumer goods becomes increasingly severe. Unless there is some kind of external force, excess capacity will inevitably bring about an economic crisis.

So how has China's economy managed to avoid such a crisis over the past almost 20 years? Or perhaps, we should ask where the complementary external buying power that could match the overcapacity — which resulted from sustained mega investment and fast-paced capacity expansion — came from? The answer: the international market. It is evident in China's continuous foreign trade surpluses from the 1990s and more than US$3 trillion in accumulated foreign reserves.[1] It is interesting to note that China's foreign trade surplus

[1] China has more than US$3 trillion in foreign reserves. Of that figure, almost US$1.6 trillion has been accumulated from direct foreign investment and other capital inflows. The amount after those figures have been deducted should be the

and forex reserves correspond precisely to the continued US foreign trade (mainly, the trade deficit with China) deficit and fiscal deficit over the same time period. In a certain sense, this provided China with a kind of exogenous and real buying power — a supernormal buying power.

The question is how has the US been able to sustain long-term trade and fiscal deficits? And what are the reasons behind?

Generally, it is difficult for a country to sustain and expand a trade deficit over a long period. But the US holds a special position. On the one hand, inadequate domestic savings and excessive consumption results in household and trade deficits. On the other hand, electoral pressures make it difficult to cut spending, while the dominance of its financial markets makes it easy to borrow money internationally. In particular, it can use the US dollar's status as the world currency to increase the supply of money to support the fiscal deficit and solve the problem, at least on the surface or temporarily. The advantage of the dollar as the world currency unfortunately has become a tool of the US Federal Reserve to excessively print the currency and support long-term debt-fuelled consumption. The result is that the US continually delays carrying out needed economic adjustments, living beyond one's means and borrowing ostentatiously. The more these kinds of unsustainable games are played, the longer they go on for, and they ultimately brought about a whole string of troubles, from the Internet bubble to the subprime mortgage crisis.

At the same time, China was adding massive amounts of new production capacity and found demand overseas. The Chinese earned massive amounts of US dollars as profits from exports. In turn, through a highly centralized foreign exchange management system, these dollars found their way back to America as a source of lending

---

foreign trade surplus, but there has already been unofficial foreign capital outflows on a major scale. Added to that has been the increasingly large official investments overseas, which has led to a massive amount of accumulated Chinese capital outflows. See China's International Investment Position as of the end of June 2011 released by the SAFE.

through the US financial markets. We could say that the economic strategies of both countries over the past more than 20 years have been inadvertently interdependent, becoming a natural pairing. For the US, Chinese exports and the returning flow of American currency is seemingly a free lunch, providing good quality yet inexpensive consumer goods for US families without causing any major political or economic impact. For China, the US market represented a third source of buying power external to its own system — a kind of supernormal purchasing power — offering real and effective demand for Chinese products, while at the same time not being a financial burden. But the US subprime mortgage crisis sparked the global financial crisis, revealing that the spontaneous economic strategic pairing of the two countries was unsustainable.

1. The Emergence and Growth of International Purchasing Power

China's high investment and overcapacity, and the excess consumption and supernormal buying power of the US are two sides of the same coin. Their emergence and development were in lock-step with each other. China's three-dimensional economic system was basically formed in the mid-1990s, at which time the impetus to drive supernormal investment was just beginning to be felt. Added to which was the reform of the forex management system and the pegging of the renminbi to the dollar, as well as China's rising investment rate, the increasing pace of capacity expansion, growth in exports and the trade surplus. Table 3.1 shows the course of this development.

It is easy to see from Table 3.1 that 1994 was the turning point for China's pattern of trade in goods. Before this time, there were alternating trade surpluses and deficits. And even in years of surplus, the scale was not very large, all under US$10 billion. After 1994, the annual trade surplus grew larger and larger. After three years, it had exceeded US$40 billion and by 2005, it had leapt over the critical US$100 billion marker to US$134.2 billion. Over the next two years,

Table 3.1 China's Trade Deficit and Growth Rate, Forex Reserves and Growth Rate for Industry Value Added 1982–2011

Year	Trade deficit (US$100 million)	Trade surplus growth (%)	Forex reserves (US$100 million)	Industry value-added growth (%)
1982	42	N/A	69.86	5.6
1983	20	-52.38	89.01	10.4
1984	0	-100.00	82.20	14.5
1985	-131	N/A	26.44	18.6
1986	-91	30.53	20.72	10.2
1987	-17	81.32	29.23	13.7
1988	-53	-211.76	33.72	14.5
1989	-56	-5.66	55.50	3.8
1990	92	264.29	110.93	3.2
1991	87	-5.43	217.12	13.9
1992	52	-40.23	194.43	21.2
1993	-107	-305.77	211.99	19.9
1994	73	168.22	516.20	18.4
1995	180	146.58	735.97	13.9
1996	195	8.33	1,050.29	12.1
1997	462	136.92	1,398.90	10.5
1998	466	0.87	1,449.59	8.9
1999	360	-22.75	1,546.75	8.1
2000	345	-4.17	1,655.74	9.4
2001	340	-1.45	2,121.65	8.4
2002	442	30.00	2,864.07	9.8
2003	444	0.45	4,032.51	12.7
2004	590	32.88	6,099.32	11.1
2005	1,342	127.46	8,188.72	12.1
2006	2,177	62.22	10,663.44	13.4
2007	3,159	45.11	15,282.49	15.1
2008	3,606	14.15	19,460.30	9.9
2009	2,495	-30.81	23,991.52	9.9
2010	2,542	1.88	28,473.38	12.3
2011	2,435	-4.21	31,811.48	10.3
Total	21,491			

Source: State Administration of Foreign Exchange Website: www.safe.gov.cn

it consecutively broke through the US$200 billion and US$300 billion marks. Between 1982 and 2011, China's accumulated surplus in its foreign trade of goods was more than US$2 trillion.

2. Asset Bubbles and Deficit Spending

In step with China's increasing trade surplus, America's household and trade deficit continued to grow in the US After the Second World War, just like in other Western countries, the US experienced a golden age of economic growth unmatched in history and there was a corresponding increase in the level of consumption. However, the rise in popularity of the welfare state, the emergence of consumer culture and the assistance of consumer credit eventually bred a generation fond of excessive consumption. This caused household spending to exceed the natural limits of what a family's income could support and created the era of household deficit spending.

After the 1980s, private consumption gradually came to assume the dominant position in the US economy, rising from about 60% of gross domestic product (GDP) before 1980 to 67% in the 1990s. In 2011, it rose again to 74%. The contribution of private consumption to GDP growth between 2000 and 2007 reached about 80%. At the same time, the growth rate of household consumption exceeded that of household income. The reason was that more and more household spending was veering toward being determined by assets, becoming a spending model based on asset-valuation. Since the 1980s, financial innovation has led to the return on assets becoming an important source of income for US households, with income from financial assets accounting for 25% of gross household earnings by 2011, up from 7% in 1950. Stocks and real estate occupy particularly important positions among the assets. In 2004, equity holdings and pensions accounted for 6% and 11%, respectively, of household assets, while real estate had jumped to more than 43%. Consequently, property and stock prices influenced the value of household assets and thereby were major factors influencing consumption.

Consumer spending brought about the "wealth effect." Statistically, an increase in residential real estate prices of 10% can cause an increase in real household spending by 1.4 percentage points. The return rate on stocks and a one-year lag in the increase in consumer spending are clearly linked, with the correlation coefficient reaching 0.44.[2] That is, even though the real scale of a household's assets, such as real estate, stocks or fund units, does not increase, as the price of the stocks and real estate and other assets climb and their market values get bigger and bigger, people will have a tendency to think there is a reason to borrow more money and lift their current level of spending. The US financial industry also designed a whole series of ways to motivate people to borrow money so they could spend. "Financial innovation" caused households to use borrowing to support their spending, especially from the 1990s onwards, when mortgages on residential properties and consumer credit were securitized. This spurred an increase in credit in the household sector and pushed up the ratio of debt in GDP. Figure 3.1 shows the rise in stock and real estate prices and the growth of debt among US households.

3. Industries Relocate Overseas and the Trade Deficit

The trouble was US household consumer deficit spending could not be completely satisfied by the output of domestic industry, resulting in reliance on imports and creating a trade deficit. In the second half of the 20th century, the international competitiveness of US industry went through a process of boom-and-bust. In the 1950s and 1960s, its competitiveness reached its peak, with the country's GDP accounting for 38% of global GDP (by 2011 that figure had dropped to 21.42%).[3] In terms of major industrial products, US steel output

[2] Bureau of Economic Analysis, "Personal Income and Outlays, October 2012," "Current Dollar and 'Real' Gross Domestic Product 2012," "'Trends in Consumer Spending and Personal Saving, 1959–2009.'"

[3] *Source*: World Bank.

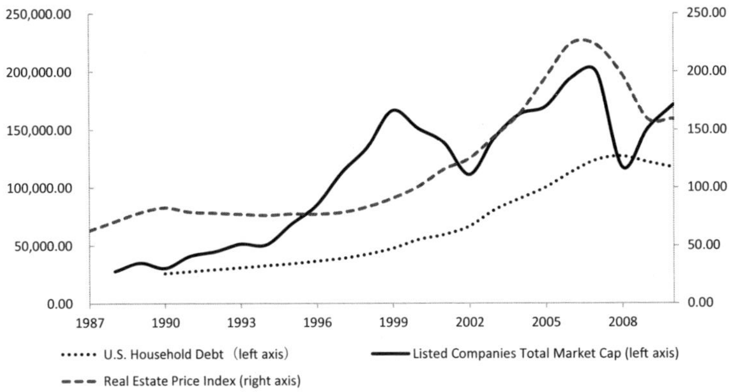

Figure 3.1 The Rise of Stock Indices and Real Estate Prices and Growth of US Household Debt (US$100 million): 1987–2012.

Source: Data on household debt prior to 1999 sourced from Federal Housing Finance Agency and only includes residential housing mortgages (http://www.fhfa.gov/Default.aspx?Page=70). Data after 1999 was sourced from the US Federal Reserve and includes total household debt (http://federalreserve.gov/econresdata/default.htm).

Data on the market capitalization of listed companies is sourced from the World Bank (http://data.worldbank.org.cn/indicator). Housing Price data from S&P/Case-Shiller Home Price Indices.

For more detailed references, see Table A.5 in the Appendix.

accounted for 47% of the global total (it fell to 11% by 1985). The scale of its manufacturing sector as a percentage of global manufacturing was at one point more than 40%.[4] Its trade in goods recorded consecutive years of surplus and reached a peak in 1964, reflecting the dominance of US manufacturing.[5] Accordingly, the US financial sector had become the unquestioned leader of the global industry. In the 1950s, two-thirds of the world's gold reserves were held by the US.[6]

As it was with other empires throughout history, reaching the peak of prosperity often signified the beginning of the downfall.

[4] IMF, World Bank: Finance and Development, December, 1987, Chinese Version.

[5] BEA, "US International Transactions from 1960–2011." Available at http://www.bea.gov/international/index.htm.

[6] World Gold Council, "Annual Time Series on World Official Gold Reserves since 1845." Available at http://www.gold.org/government_affairs/gold_reserves/.

After the Second World War and facing the rise of the Soviet Union, the US started planning for the rebuilding of Western Europe's economy as well as stabilizing and supporting the Japanese economy. The Marshall Plan contributed to the recovery of the European economy and General Douglas Macarthur's governance over Japan stabilized its economy and society. The outbreak of the Korean War gave the Japanese economy an opportunity for a new start and from this point, the industrial economies of Western Europe and Japan developed at a sustained rapid pace. At that time, Western Europe, the US and Japan experienced the most rapid and stable period of development seen in the modern era, described by many scholars as the Golden Age of Capitalism. But by comparison, many areas of industry in Western Europe and Japan began to surpass their counterparts in the US, posing a challenge to America. Starting with the capital-intensive industries of steel, shipbuilding and vehicle production, the competitiveness of Western Europe and Japan began to gradually erode the dominance of US industries in these sectors.

After the oil crisis in the 1970s, the US car industry failed to come up with a response to the energy shortage and therefore quickly fell behind its counterparts in Japan and Western Europe. The comprehensive and rapid rise of the Japanese car industry opened the door for the decline of US carmakers. At this time, the major cities in the Great Lakes region of the US had to undergo a painful transition due to the loss of their core competitiveness. In addition, the luxury goods industries in France and Italy among others were becoming competitive and even surpassing those in the US. It was the first wave of challenges for US industry.

After this, there was the rise of the "Four Asian Tigers." These economies had undergone an upgrade from labor-intensive to capital-intensive. After the Asian Financial Crisis, South Korea, Singapore and Taiwan all succeeded in structural transformation. A certain number of key industrial sectors transformed from extensive management to innovation-driven management based on information economy. The electronics and information technology industries in particular threatened the core competitiveness of the US tech sector. In Taiwan, industry players first entered into strategic cooperation with brand enterprises in the US, building a global industrial network. As this process deepened, more and more of Taiwan's own brands emerged, and they competed with each other as well as with established international brands in the global marketplace.

This was followed by China, India, Brazil and other emerging economies, whose mid- to low-end industries not only had a major impact on the US, but also Western Europe and Japan. As the emerging economies developed, their industrial structures gradually moved toward high-end, creating additional pressure and difficulty for US manufacturers, more and more of whom weakened and stagnated. But, US economic strategic policy decisions failed to keep up with the times. Not only did the US not make any substantive effort to revitalize the real economy, it tried virtualizing the financial industry and played games with money as means of support. On the one hand, as domestic social welfare leads to excessive consumption and becomes a political demand that must be respected, all kinds of interest groups are indulged in raising the costs of aged pensions, education and medical treatment among other kinds of social welfare benefits. This leads to a comprehensive jump in costs of labor and the legal industries and a further deterioration in competitiveness for more and more US sectors.

Under this type of pressure, some US enterprises moved toward failure, while a few others with a global outlook and ability drew support from the wave of globalization and separated out their manufacturing and design departments and moved their manufacturing operations to the emerging economies. The result was that the profitability of these enterprises became stronger and they have become global industrial giants who utilize the world's resources to realize sustained growth. However, it also led to the hollowing out of most US industries.

Correspondingly, China, India and other emerging economies took advantages of their own comparative competitive advantages and participated in the global competition by their increasingly upgrading industrial sectors. Thus, they accumulated large trade

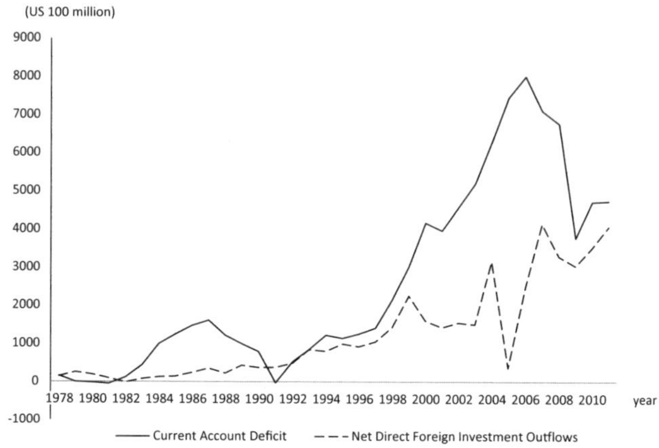

Figure 3.2 Annual US Capital Outflows and the Trade Deficit 1978–2011 (US$100 million).

Source: World Bank http://data.worldbank.org.cn/indicator. For more detailed references, see Table A.6 in the Appendix.

surpluses and brought down global prices. Although the US can temporarily rely on its financial industry to maintain its national power, enterprises gained room for growth through manipulating industrial capital which was transferred offshore and deployed around the globe. But over the long-term, it weakened the real US economy and caused a continued increase in its trade deficit. Figure 3.2 shows the relationship between the outflows of US capital and the trade deficit over the past more than 30 years.

4. Fiscal Deficit and Excessive Issuance of US Dollars

The cause of the US household and trade deficits was also the reason behind the national fiscal deficit. The groups of people who indulge in excessive consumption are usually the ones who are always demanding more spending on social welfare. Through the process of electoral politics, these types of demands often become ingrained fiscal expenditures that continually increase. The origin of the trade deficit is the stagnation and decline of industry, which implies a sluggish jobs market and an increase in the amount of people receiving welfare payments. It also indicates lacklustre corporate investment and a falling capability to pay taxes. So as fiscal expenditure increases, income falls, resulting in an expanding fiscal deficit.

But who picks up the tab for the deficit? As the household and industrial sectors both already have deficits, the only way out is through financial means and currency issuance. Consequently, the US financial industry became very advanced and the dollar is the world currency. And thus, as demand creates supply, from the 1980s, the US issuance of dollars started upon a track of long-term growth. The question is how can they keep issuing such large amounts of dollars? Under the Bretton Woods system, the dollar and gold were directly linked, whereby the amount of dollar holdings equalled an equivalent amount of gold holdings. But in 1971, the administration of President Richard Nixon, compelled by the declining US economy and gold reserves that could not support the supply of dollars, decided to end the convertibility of dollars to gold.

After this decoupling, the dollar became the fiduciary currency issued by the US. If there is an excessive issuance of dollars, in accordance with basic economics, it will cause the currency to depreciate and fuel domestic inflation. (Indeed, at times when they decided) to de-couple the dollar and gold, the US authorities had been worried about the above scenario occurring. The reasoning was very simple: prior to de-coupling, holding dollars was the equivalent to holding gold, and therefore the dollar was the international currency. After de-coupling, as the dollar was just a paper currency issued by the US, why should people still choose to hold it?

To solve this problem, they must ensure that the dollar is the only internationally accepted hard currency and that trade settlements between countries would only be conducted in dollars. In this way, the dollar would have a monopoly on the purchase of goods internationally and thus lead to central banks of all nations building a reserve of dollars to ensure the stability of their economies.

Additionally, after such a large issuance of dollars, they must make certain that this currency can not find its way back into the US economic system to ensure that domestic prices will not be affected. So after the de-coupling of the dollar and gold, the most important thing was to maintain US dollar's position as global currency with effective international buying power and to create new and unceasingly growing demand for US dollar. From this perspective, US strategic decision-making had achieved a great success. First, the US controlled the market supply of some very important strategic commodities, such as oil, making it possible to use the dollar as a hard currency. Second, it created the Eurodollar market to absorb the massive amount of excess dollars generating from global oil trading and to keep these dollars in Europe. Of course, ultimately, those who hold dollars must be able to receive profits and governments must be able to nominally maintain and increase the value of their dollar holdings. By ensuring this, governments and central banks will "voluntarily" hold dollar reserves that far exceed the demands of their domestic economies. So apart from paying the interest on the US government bonds, it also created a conditional guarantee that these bonds could be bought and sold at any time and could be easily liquidated. This also created a need for a large-scale financial product exchange market so any economic entity that is holding US government bonds could trade them at any time on a bond market. In line with this, different types of US assets could be traded in the market, where prices would rise and fall, completing the mystical process whereby the dollar moved from being just a paper currency to an object of value. From this, we can see that the ultimate guarantee of maintaining a paper currency's value when a monstrous amount of dollars was issued, is a large-scale financial exchange.

Indeed, the scale of the financial revolution at the time was massive, the products were complex and the financial market was multilayered. This allowed the dollar to hold on to its position as the international currency for decades. As part of this process, the US Fed issued dollars and gave them to the Treasury Department, which was then in debt to the Fed. Later, the liquidity was injected into the US economy by fiscal expenditure and monetary market manipulations. The Fed could also use different types of channels to move dollars into the banking system and the banks could use their financial operations to create dollar inflows into the economy. So the multilayered financial market could injected liquidity which created by Fed into the global economy by bond issuance and trading. In this dazzling financial market, the complexity of trading resulted in financial asset prices to ebb and flow, allowing the dollar to have an independent worth, like a valuable commodity such as oil or precious metals. This completed the process of the US dollar going from being just a symbol on a banknote to the reality of being something with real value.

Thus, despite the global hegemony of the US financial industry, as well as its complexities and mystical manipulative abilities, this kind of unquenchable fetish for dollars could not go on forever. In fact, the expansion of the financial industry is the inevitable product of maintaining the hegemonic position of the US economy amid its own decline.

So from the 1980s, the US began the so-called "financial engineering" of the virtual economy revolution that developed rapidly. When the global financial crisis broke out in 2008, the scale of the derivative products market was already sky high. From Figure 3.3, we can see that the growth in US derivatives as part of the new virtual economy not only far exceeded that of GDP in the real economy, but also left the traditional virtual economy such as stocks and bonds far, far behind.

The growth rate of financial assets greatly exceeded that of the national economy, expanding to US$67 trillion by 2011 from US$10 trillion in 1986. Figure 3.4 shows how most of the impetus for growth came from the expanding scale of over-the-counter products: They just began in 2000, reached almost 10 trillion in 2004 and surpassed 27 trillion in 2011.

Growth was especially fast in the capital markets and the financial derivatives sectors, increasingly lifting their status in the US economy. Figure 3.5 shows how the proportion of financial industry's profit to US national profit went up from 10% in 1940', to 15% in 1985 and then to 30.59% by 2000.

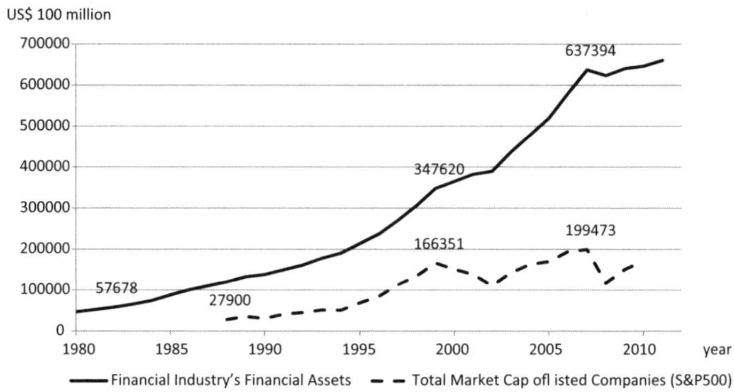

Figure 3.3 Expansion of the US Financial Industry 1980–2011 (US$100 million).
Source: World Bank, US Bureau of Economic Analysis (BEA). For more detailed references, see Table A.7 in the Appendix.

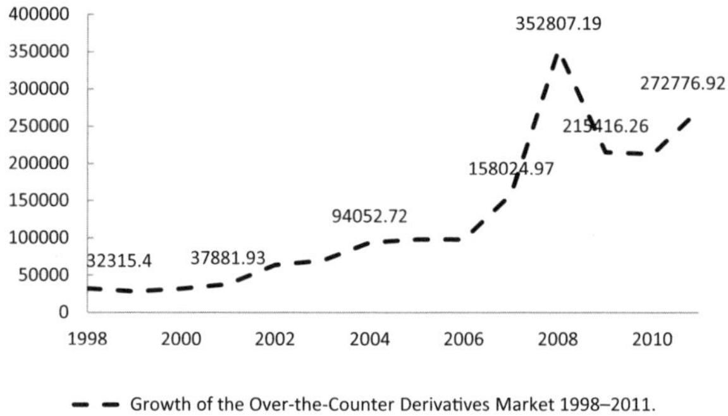

Figure 3.4 Growth of the Over-the-Counter Derivatives Market 1998–2011. Market Value (US$100 million).
Source: Bank for International Settlements (http://www.bis.org/statistics/derstats.htm). For more detailed references, see Table A.7 in the Appendix.

It is worth considering that the strong growth of the US financial industry did not bring about a revitalization of the real economy, but it did create essential market conditions for the excessive printing of dollars. However, as the "autonomy" of dollar issuance gave the US government the freedom to extend the fiscal deficit, in turn, it also postponed the determination of US society and government to solve the deficit. The result was issuance of US dollars and the fiscal

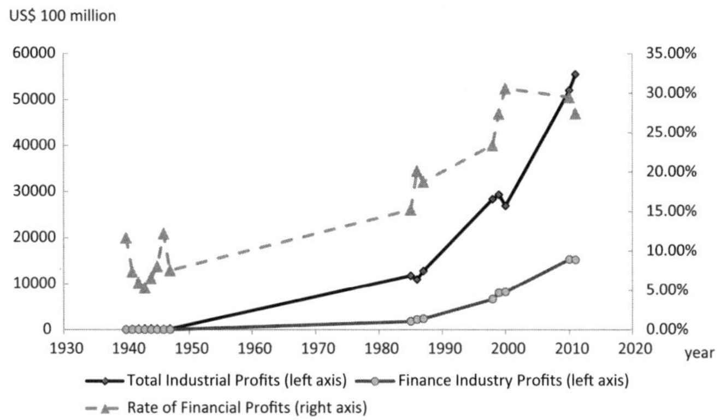

Figure 3.5 US Financial and Industry Profits 1940–2011 (US$100 million).

Note: Finance industry includes financing, insurance and banking and other holding companies. *Source*: US Bureau of Economic Analysis (BEA) http://www.bea.gov/. For more detailed references, see Table A.8 in the Appendix.

deficit advanced hand in hand right up to the point where they got out of hand.

5. The Limits and Crisis of Supernormal Purchasing Power

In summary, a major precondition of China achieving supernormal growth was the existence of extraordinary purchasing power. But this buying power was reliant on three major US deficits: spending deficit by the household deficit, trade deficit by the industry and fiscal deficit by the government. And in the final analysis, these occurred against a backdrop of excessive dollar issuance. Clearly, this deficit-driven economic model based on excessive currency issuance cannot be sustainable. In 2007, the US subprime crisis was quickly spreading to engulf the world in financial turmoil, which subsequently evolved into a protracted economic downturn. This officially heralded the bankrupting of the US economic deficit model and also implied that the reliance of China's supernormal growth model on the international market environment had changed.

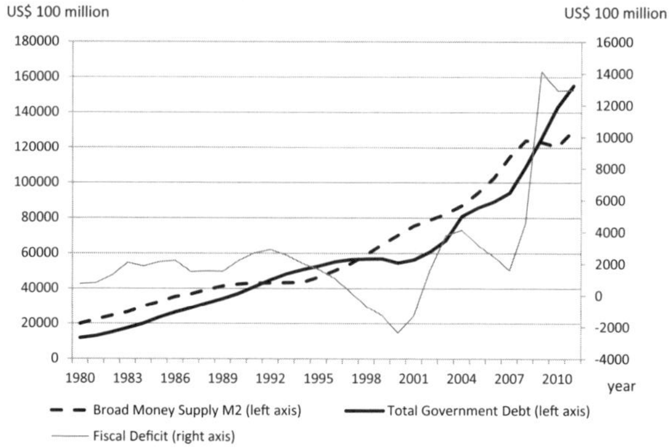

Figure 3.6 Value of US Dollar Issuance and the Deficit 1980–2011 (US$100 million).
Source: Congressional Budget Office, IMF, World Bank. For more detailed references, see Table A.9 in the Appendix.

We could say that over the past more than 30 years, China and the US both have been implementing imbalanced developmental strategies. China had pursued imbalanced fast-paced high growth, a characteristic of which is the so-called "three lows, three highs":

Low Wages — Low Consumption Ratio — Low Domestic Market Demand

High Investment — High Growth — High Foreign Trade Surplus

The US on the other hand maintained an imbalanced deficit-driven economy, which can be summarized thus:

Low Investment — Low Growth — High Foreign Trade Deficit

High Asset Bubbles — High Consumption — High Household Deficit

The development of the Chinese and US economies had unintentionally become a strategic complementary pairing, with each equally reliant on the other and mutually indispensable. The internal logic of this spontaneous strategic pairing is evident. On the one hand, China swaps its resources and products in exchange for dollars and the real economy was able to see long-term development,

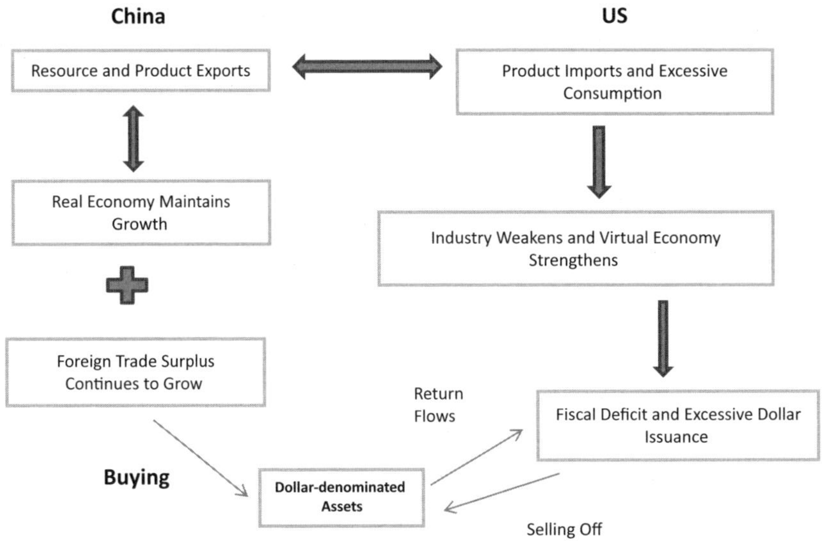

Figure 3.7 China–US Strategic Pairing.

but it also meant accumulating a pile of continually depreciating US dollars. On the other hand, the US relied on printing dollars to sustain its deficit and domestic consumer welfare, damaging the real economy and causing it to become increasingly virtualized.

The characteristic of this strategic pairing was that both sides were imbalanced and the long-term consequence was that these two countries brought this imbalance to the global economy. Currently, the economic strategies of both the US and China are facing challenges. In some sense, China and the US are the biggest beneficiaries of this process of globalization. But the strengthening trend of China's real economy and the US virtual economy to a certain extent is already difficult to sustain. The reason the US trend is unsustainable is that the real economy always has to maintain a certain scale and after all, virtual economies and asset bubbles will ultimately burst. Under current conditions, China's is also unsustainable because the risk of continuing to keep using scarce resources and products to swap for large amounts of dollars becomes more and more difficult to bear. At the same time, the global economy does not have the power to endure the consequences of the long-term imbalances of these two large economies.

The crisis is forcing the world economy to enter a period of major adjustment. China's imbalanced strategic growth of the "three lows, three highs" and the US development model of the household, trade and fiscal deficits, or "three deficits," are facing fundamental transformations. The relationship between the management models of these two major economies must be radically rebuilt. Importantly, the healthy, long-term development of the world economy is dependent upon whether China and the US can concurrently and successfully transform their strategies and models. There is no doubt that implementing the concurrent transformation of development strategy and economic models of these two countries are an unprecedented challenge.

Chapter 4

A New Historical Phase for China's Economic Growth

China's economic development is entering a new phase after more than 30 years of supernormal growth. Over this period, both domestic and external environments have undergone remarkable change. On the demand side, the financial crisis sweeping the world has heralded the end of supernormal international purchasing power. On the supply side, bottlenecks in the availability of various factors of production are becoming increasingly severe, with the constraints on the ecological environment, energy, resources, human capital and technological innovation posing a critical challenge to China's economic growth. So the question is: can China's supernormal growth model continue to work?

First, let us look at the demand side. The scale of future economic growth depends on the gap between the developed and the underdeveloped areas. China is still a major developing country with per capita income at mid-level or below when compared to the world average. Development in China's eastern coastal areas, where 500 million people live and work, has reached a primary level of modernization. However, in the vast central and western areas, development has only just begun.[1]

[1] National Bureau of Statistics of China, "China Statistical Yearbook 2012," China Statistics Press, 2012.

Evidently, it will require decades of further growth before China is fully modernized and its billions of people are living prosperous and civilized lives. Therefore, the need for long-term growth is imperative. But the question is how to turn potential demand into real demand? The core of the problem is finding an alternative to supernormal purchasing power. China could only sustain conventional economic growth if there was no effective substitute for the US Fed-backed supernormal international purchasing power. Therefore, finding a substitute is the key to maintaining China's supernormal growth.

Second, the supply side. According to the modern theory of economic growth, the rate of long-term economic expansion depends on the growth rate of the nation's capital, labor and factor productivity. If the growth rate of factor productivity remains unchanged, then the investment rate will directly determine the economic growth rate.[2] At present, excessive savings and investment rates are among the major problems facing China. Thus, there is no shortage in capital supply for economic growth. The key is how to convert the nation's savings into effective investment and solving the bottlenecks in resources and environment. In the long run, the constraints in the factors of production pose both challenges and opportunities, pointing to the direction of future development. Meeting the challenges means opening up new room for growth. In fact, solutions can be found for all the problems in energy and resources, ecological environment and population quality with the current level of technology available. The crucial requirement for solving these issues is a huge amount of capital. Thus, the real difficulty lies in how to arrange these massive investments.

---

[2] The so-called modern growth theory refers to the economic growth model put forward by Nobel Prize laureate Robert M. Solow in 1957 after the Harrod–Domar growth model was developed by Roy F. Harrod in 1939 and Evsey Domar in 1946. Since then, many scholars have expanded Solow's model, proposing a multi-sector growth model, but the significance is unclear. Robert E. Lucas (2009), also a Nobel Prize laureate, and Paul M. Romer (1986) developed the new growth theory, adding knowledge and technological advances as the key factors stimulating growth.

We can see that the demand and supply side challenges of long-term growth are contradictory. On the one hand, diminishing supernormal international purchasing power results in a lack of effective demand and excessive savings. On the other hand, solutions to bottlenecks in various factors of production and ecological and environmental issues must contend with an insufficient supply of funds. Therefore, an appropriate mechanism to pair investment growth in the bottlenecked supply side with the excessive savings of the demand side must be explored.

In fact, the current under-consumption and overcapacity is just a temporal phenomenon. Only the conventional manufacturing sectors have experienced overcapacity. And here, consumption only refers to that of the household sector, namely spending on food, clothing, housing and transport. Once new variables are introduced, such as consumption expansion, consumption and industrial upgrades, urban development, ecological construction, environmental protection, a shift in energy consumption and human resource development, the room for future joint growth of consumption and investment will be tremendous.

1. Upgrading Consumption and Industry

Gaining a comprehensive and accurate understanding of the structure of future consumption, and thereby also an appreciation of the corresponding framework of investment and industry, is vital to the upgrade of consumption and industry.

(1) *Basic Consumption*

Basic consumption refers to consumer spending closely related to people's basic living standards, normally covering food, clothing, housing, transport and other activities related to population reproduction. In the process of economic development, the scope of basic consumption will expand accordingly and will inevitably include training and education, medical care, entertainment and recreation, and tourism among others. In fact, China's domestic consumption has undergone sustained, stable and rapid growth since reform and opening up in the late 1970s, with more robust growth seen since the second half of the 1990s. Although the consumption-to-GDP ratio fell considerably in the early days and during some periods of the reforms, the consumption growth rate started to accelerate as waves of investment in large-scale heavy industry gradually stabilized. Over at least the past 10 years, China's total retail sales of consumer goods have been growing in line with the increase in GDP.[3]

In terms of purchasing power, the premise for growth and expansion of basic consumption is an increase in household income. This is an issue of income distribution. However, when we look at the components of consumption, we notice that the income to be distributed must first be generated. Therefore, production growth, or investment growth, is indispensable to effecting an increase in consumption. For example, in order to increase per capita consumption of food, such as flour, grains, edible oil, vegetables, meat, eggs, milk and tea, the overall production of these foodstuffs must be expanded. As a result, investment in irrigation, soil, fertilizers and labor will need to be increased accordingly. Furthermore, infrastructure investment in land reclamation and farmland improvement will be essential.

Housing is another example. The formation of China's affordable housing system indicates that the country has included the right to housing as one of the basic social consumption needs of the people. According to traditional Chinese values, owning a home is a basic need. In the experience of modern economic growth, the majority of people having a stable job and owning a home are prerequisites for a nation to enjoy stable and long-term economic development. In a market economy, housing has the dual functions of being both consumption and investment. And where there is

[3]According to the "Statistical Communiqué on the National Economic and Social Development" released annually by the National Bureau of Statistics, in the past 10 years, the real average growth rate of China's total retail sales of social consumer goods was 15.65%, higher than China's real GDP growth during the same period.

investment, there is bound to be speculation and market bubbles. If housing was solely reliant on the spontaneous operation of the real estate market, there inevitably would be a considerable number of low-income groups that would not be able to resolve their housing problems. Assuming that China's population will eventually reach 1.5 billion, even if only 30% of that number are middle- and low-income groups, massive funding will be required to house them as part of the nation's affordable housing scheme. In addition to the mammoth investment, there will be unlimited opportunities to develop the building materials and construction sectors.

The nation's compulsory education and free basic healthcare programs are facing similar issues. In practice, few nations have completely turned to the market mechanism to provide funding for these two sectors. As a socialist country, China should assume more of the obligation and thus secure funding for them. Naturally enough, these obligations will require increasing the number of schools and hospitals and adding more teachers and doctors. Again, this will need a huge investment. Over the long-term, consumption of basic living essentials as well as the required production and investment are, in fact, different aspects of the same process.

(2) *Consumption Upgrade*

In addition to the growth and expansion of basic consumption, an upgrade will become another driving force for the long-term future growth of consumption. And the major battleground for a consumption upgrade will be among the middle class and the relatively wealthy. Currently, along with their proportion to the overall population, the number of middle-and-high income individuals is growing at a relatively fast pace. It is estimated that this group will reach between 500 million and 1 billion in the future, indicating that consumption has immeasurable room for growth. But currently, segments of the relatively high-end purchasing power in China have flowed into the international market, while other segments cannot be realized and therefore are constrained. In addition to traditional import products like brand-name garments, jewellery, watches, cosmetics and high-end cars, other once less internationally sought after categories like food, milk powder, educational and medical services have been added in significant quantities to the shopping lists of Chinese buyers.

China is exporting its domestic purchasing power to the international market on a massive scale and the trend is increasing, as shown by the "shopping sprees" for international goods of outbound mainland China tourists, international purchases via the Internet and the constant cross-border buying between Hong Kong and Guangdong. According to data from the China National Tourism Administration, outbound tourists reached 70.25 million in 2011, an increase of 22.4% compared with the previous year.[4] In the same year, overseas spending by Chinese travelers reached US$72.6 billion, or about RMB450 billion.[5] For spending on services, we can take the education sector as an example. According to the "Blue Book of Global Talent: Annual Report on Chinese Students Studying Abroad 2012," the number of Chinese students overseas reached 339,700 in 2011, accounting for 14% of the global number of international students, the largest in the world.[6] Assuming annual expenditure of RMB300,000 per student, the outflow of China's educational spending was more than RMB100 billion. In the healthcare sector, the scale of medical tourism as well as that of the services provided by professional consulting agencies to facilitate outbound travel for medical care is constantly expanding.

The relatively inferior quality, brand recognition and service in China's domestic high-end consumer industry is the root cause behind such a tremendous portion of Chinese consumer spending ending up in the international market. Although China's manufacturing sector has made remarkable advances, the improvement in

[4] China National Tourism Administration, "China Tourism Statistics Bulletin 2012," October 2012.

[5] State Administration of Foreign Exchange, "2011 China International Balance of Payments."

[6] Wang Huiyao (ed.), "Blue Book of Global Talent: Annual Report on Chinese Students Studying Abroad 2012," Social Sciences Academic Press (China), 2012.

quality of "Made in China" products has not been proportional to the expansion in scale. Currently, Chinese manufacturers still cannot independently produce the core components used in high-end cars, cameras and some electronic products, or make devices like sophisticated medical apparatus or even environmentally-friendly flooring and insulating glass. Some industries whose manufacturing technology is world class, such as the textile and garment sectors, cannot provide high value-added products for consumers with large incomes due to lack of brand appeal. To make matters worse, insufficient regulation in certain industries has caused significant product safety problems, intensifying the irrational trust domestic consumers place in international goods and spurring imports.

In order to meet domestic consumers' increasing demand for quality products and services and reverse the massive outflow of domestic buying power, great effort must be made to lift the standards of the consumer industry. This is also a prerequisite for upgrading consumption. Enhancement of the consumer industry will inevitably involve a comprehensive improvement of equipment, materials, technologies and management of related sectors, otherwise a consumption upgrade will be impossible. That is to say, the consumption upgrade itself involves the urgent expansion of the scale of industry and building up the industrial chain. Increasing investment will be an indispensable factor in all of the above tasks.

(3) *Industrial Upgrade*

A consumption upgrade requires lifting the standards of the consumer goods industry. To do so, it is essential to enhance the related sectors that provide the means of production for this industry. Both basic consumption and a consumption upgrade will place higher requirements on industries like equipment makers, materials and logistics, which cannot be met without advancement in science and technology as well as investment. The government's national development plan identified seven strategic emerging industries as priority development objectives, undoubtedly a choice made with a mind to their role in China's overall development strategy. They are also key to determining China's global economic competitiveness in the coming decades.[7] In addition to the objectives of the selected strategic emerging industries, there are two other important tasks as part of this industrial upgrade: (1) taking advantage of advances in informationalization and new materials to systematically transform the traditional industries and comprehensively improve their products and efficiency in resource utilization and reduce their pollution. This will be a very involving and arduous task; (2) adapt and guide the consumption upgrade, and develop multilayered consumption industry clusters in a timely manner and at a high level, especially in modern services industries like education, health, entertainment and leisure travel. If breakthroughs in technology are crucial for the development of strategic emerging industries, then solutions to institutional and management issues are essential to the transformation of the traditional industries and the consumption upgrade. If the institutional issues can be dealt with steadfastly, then expansion into new growth territories will pick up significant momentum.

It should be emphasized that the main target area for an industrial upgrade should be the manufacturing sector. As China's manufacturing industry is huge in scale and standards have seen significant long-term cumulative improvement, some experts and scholars proposed replacing the catchphrase "Made in China" with "Created in China." This proposal is in line with the central government's major strategy of building an innovation-driven nation. However, if "creation" is defined as making breakthroughs from scratch in new products or new technologies at the forefront of the

[7]The seven strategic emerging industries refer to seven areas (23 key directions) identified to receive support policies issued by central and local governments. The seven industries include energy-saving and environmental protection, next-generation information technology, biotechnology, new energy, new-energy vehicles, advanced equipment manufacturing and new materials. See "The 12th Five-Year Plan for the Development of National Strategic Emerging Industries" issued by the State Council.

global field in science, then this kind of "creation" will not play a central role in the upgrading of China's manufacturing industry for a very long time. The reason for this is that the main issues for most sectors in the industry — such as steel, machinery, materials and automobiles — are not creating new products, but upgrading current manufacturing standards to advanced international levels in order to enhance technologies, as well as building their brand and increasing value.

Take the automobile industry for example: domestically-made vehicles of home-grown brands can rarely be sold for more than RMB200,000, with manufacturers experiencing relative overcapacity and extremely low margins. In contrast, luxury vehicles, almost all of which are foreign brands, can easily be sold for more than a million renminbi and still bring in huge margins, and market demand is booming. Similar examples can be found in almost every manufacturing sector and this kind of disparity can be attributed to the fundamental gap in manufacturing standards. In fact, between creation and manufacturing, there is another category: precision manufacturing. Chinese manufacturers should first enter the field of precision manufacturing. In coming decades, the theme for China's industrial upgrade should be "From Made-in-China to Precision Manufactured in China." Achieving this will inevitably require comprehensive improvement in equipment, materials, quality of labor and management and consequentially involve massive long-term capital accumulation, including investment in human capital and physical capital.

It is worth noting that the above issues involved in the upgrades to consumption and industry are also relevant to the "middle income trap," a current hot topic. The so-called "middle income trap" was initially put forward by the World Bank in its East Asian Economic Development Report (2006). It refers to a stage in economic development where a country's per capita GDP is unable to break through the US$10,000 level for a sustained period of time after working its way out of the "poverty trap" (per capita GDP of less than US$1,000) and heading into the "economic take-off" stage (per capita GDP of between US$1,000 and US$3,000). It often stagnates at a mid-level between US$3,000 and US$5,000.[8] Thus, the World Bank believes that the development strategies and growth mechanisms employed at the "take-off" stage of a country's economy cannot be adopted in the process of transforming from a middle-income economy to a high-income economy.

Discussion on the aforementioned "middle income trap" do not provide an explanation for why a country struggles for so long at this income level. The "middle income trap" is in fact an "industry structure" trap.[9] If a country's industrial structure remains stalled at middle or lower levels and cannot be upgraded, then it will not be able to provide products and services for domestic high-end consumers. This is bound to cause an outflow of domestic buying power. Furthermore, reliance on the international market to satisfy domestic high-end consumption in turn prevents the formation of related industrial clusters at home. With the relative absence of high-end industries, there will be a dearth of high-income jobs, which will hold back the formation of a domestic middle class. Against this backdrop, it is extremely easy to form *social income distribution trap.* According to the Kuznets Curve theory, in the early economic take-off period, income distribution would deteriorate; with the transition from middle income to high income, distribution would improve.[10] However, if the industrial structure is stagnating, the improvement in income distribution will also be stagnant, cementing a state of inequitable income distribution. Consequently, it will lead to social instability, which in turn discourages entrepreneurship, investment and industrial upgrades. Therefore, if we trace its origin, the so-called "middle income trap" is essentially a trap of the industrial upgrade and income inequality, which is the outcome of a nation's inability to develop independently. For China, it is crucial to improve

---

[8] Indermit Gill *et al.*, An East Asian Renaissance: Ideas for Economic Growth, World Bank Publications, 2007.

[9] This point of view was formed when the author held a discussion with Yin Tongyue, Chairman of Cherry Automobile, in Shanghai.

[10] Simon Kuznets, "Economic Growth and Income Inequality," *American Economic Review*, 1955, Vol. 5, pp. 1–28.

the nation's capacity for independent development and continue to promote industrial upgrades.

2. Urbanization

Continual progress made in industrial upgrading and industrialization will certainly provide a solid and sustained base for China's urbanization and hopefully help the nation avoid the setbacks widely witnessed during the course of urbanization in Latin American countries. Against this backdrop, the scale and pace of China's urbanization will depend on the size and pace of rural–urban migration. It is estimated that roughly 30% of China's 700 million urban dwellers, or around 200 million people, are migrant workers who have not been truly assimilated into the urban population.[11] On the other hand, assuming that China's population will eventually reach 1.5 billion and the total rural population will be 400 million, there could be 300 million people joining the rural–urban migration. Thus, there could be 300 million to 500 million rural migrants who become urban residents and modern consumers over the next two decades. On a macro level, it would be like creating another US.[12]

Housing such a large newly urbanized population will require the construction of around 100 million new residential units, as well as the provision of municipal educational, medical, cultural and other public services and facilities. The demand for infrastructure will be astronomical. Additionally, the new urban citizens will bring sustained demand for goods and services providing an enormous boost to existing urban consumption. Therefore, it is realistic and

[11] "The 6th National Population Census of the People's Republic of China," released by National Bureau of Statistics in 2010, shows that the population residing in urban areas reached 666 million, while the population not residing in their household registration areas — excluding those not residing in their registration area but within the same city-level jurisdiction — reached 221 million.

[12] In 2010, the US population was 308 million, according to the "Resident Population Data: Population Change," released by the US Census Bureau in 2010.

feasible for urbanization to serve as the main driving force for China's economy for a long time into the future.

However, there are a number of issues that need properly addressing in the ongoing process of urbanization, such as the disproportionate levels of development among large, medium and small-sized cities, urbanization of the land faster than that of the population, uneven progress in the process of rural migrants becoming city dwellers, and, in recent years, the "forced urbanization" of farmers in some regions. Effective resolution of these issues will add momentum for sustained economic growth in China.

3. Ecology and Environment

(1) *Ecological Construction*

For a nation's people, standard of living, quality of life and degree of happiness depend not only on private consumption by households, but also on the public consumption by society. In public consumption, special importance is attached to the ecological and environmental consumption, which is highly relevant to China's national conditions.

The ecological environment is the origin of a nation's physical existence. It is also the most primitive and basic source of consumable materials. When people's basic needs such as food, clothing, housing and transportation have been fulfilled, elements in the ecological environment such as blue skies, green spaces, clean water, fresh air and quiet streets — all of which have the greatest possible prevention and control capabilities against natural disasters and large-scale epidemic outbreaks — become important components in determining their happiness index. However, the status of the ecological assets held by the contemporary Chinese people is worrisome. Even though China's land area is vast, snow-covered plateaus, the Gobi Desert, and barren wastelands account for more than half of the landscape; there are the glacial meltwaters that feed into the Yangze River and Yellow River that run through the country, but the available water resources per capita are at crisis levels; over the long run, the South-to-North

Water Transfer Project will eventually run dry; and while it is true that China has the world's most diverse and exotic scenery, there are numerous natural disasters due to the combined effects of China's topography (high in the west and low in the east) and its special atmospheric circulation, which causes floods and drought to occur in the same season. Typhoons, earthquakes, landslides and dust storms are constant threats. Therefore, in China, high-quality ecological and environmental consumption must be a result of the long-term accumulation of ecological assets. This can be achieved in two ways: (1) comprehensive land improvement. This will involve improving the nation's mountains, water, farmland, forests, highways, mines and cities, all of which will pose challenges; (2) climate amelioration. The crux is to change the geographical distribution of rainfall, turning the vast desert areas in the northwest region into fertile lands as a permanent cure for desertification. This will be an even more challenging and difficult task. In addition to employing technology, tremendous amounts of investment will be needed. Simply put, investment must be made before the nation can accumulate any ecological assets. The level of public consumption of the ecological environment depends on the level of the nation's investment. Consumption is an investment — this is the rationale of the ecological economy.

(2) *Environmental Protection*

In the past more than 30 years, continuous high-speed economic growth has created unprecedented pressure on the environment. Pollution has worsened compared with the early days of reform and opening up and some major environmental incidents have severely affected people's health. To some extent, China's fast-paced development has come at a tremendous cost to the environment. However, we should note that in recent years, the state has placed greater emphasis and taken more concrete action on environmental protection. Thanks to industrial upgrades, the increasing use of clean energy, the research, development and promotion of new technologies to boost efficiency, as well as implementation of environmental laws and policies, controls on industrial pollution have clearly been effective and the momentum behind most of the pollution brought into check. However, when taking into account long-term economic growth over the coming decades, the main pollutants accumulated during that period will have catastrophic consequences for the nation's ecology over time, even though the overall emission of pollutants is controllable or on the decline. Thus, exploratory work needs to be done with a new vision that transcends the conventional concept of economic costs in order to foster fast-paced growth built on the long-term health and development of the nation.

In 2010, the State Council issued the "Decision on Accelerating the Cultivation and Development of Strategic Emerging Industries," in which energy conservation and environmental protection was made the principal industry among the other six sectors. At the same time, the new energy and new-energy vehicle industries, which have the greatest influence on the environment, were also included in the list. This signaled the high strategic importance being placed on the environmental protection industry in China. Again, the main problem with environmental protection is not technological, it is investment. It requires an effective one-time capital investment to promote advances in technologies related to energy conservancy and environmental protection. This will ultimately raise the level of the circular economy, not only reducing overall emissions of pollutants, but also eventually leading to emissions that are harmless. In other words, the energy-saving and environmental protection industry will become mainstream with huge potential, supporting the sustainable development of society as a whole.

4. Energy and Resources

It is often said that China is a vast country with abundant resources. However, it is actually resource poor in per capita terms. As summarized by Professor Deng Yingtao,[13] except for tungsten and rare

[13] Deng Yingtao, "Zaizao Zhongguo, Zouxiang Weilai [Rebuilding China Into the Future]," Shanghai People's Press, 2013, pp. 241–242.

earth, of which China has rich reserves, other main resources per capita are far below the world average, such as arable land (equivalent to 30% of the world average), forests (13%), grasslands (33%), fresh water (24%), coal (47%), oil (32–64%), hydroelectric energy (61%), iron ore (48%), aluminum (33%) and copper (29%). On top of this, the quality of the resources is inferior and some have been seriously degraded. For example, China lacks large-scale high-grade copper and iron ore mines; the coal reserves have a high sulfur content; the degradation rate of grassland is more than 80% and only less than 2% of the nation's overall grassland have been ameliorated with manmade turf; forestry resources are low-grade with the majority made up of young forests and woodlands; degraded land resources account for nearly 60% of China's total land area due to various types of erosion, keeping the productivity and value of the land low. Meanwhile, the structural imbalance among resources, population and production capacity is worsening. Approximately, 90% of the population and industrial production capacity has been congested into the eastern side of the Heihe–Tengchong Line (a hypothetical line that starts from Heihe in Heilongjiang Province and runs diagonally down to Tengchong County in Yunnan Province, dividing the nation in two equal parts), while more than half of the nation's resources are distributed on the western side of the line, which is home to less than 10% of the population and industrial production capacity. This structural imbalance has led to a decrease in the accessibility to resources, with high overland transport costs for the long distances causing a loss in its economic utilization value and possibly further lowering the nation's level of resources per capita. And as China's energy demand will grow along with progress in industrialization and urbanization, shortages of energy and other resources would pose an extremely serious problem for sustaining future growth, with energy security becoming a critical issue.

(1) *Energy Transformation*

Energy is one of the top issues for China's future growth. The government is aiming to achieve full modernization by 2050, when per capita

GDP is targeted have reached the level of developed countries. In order to accomplish this goal, per capita energy consumption and the nation's total energy demand will inevitably increase many times over. Fundamentally speaking, the high levels of per capita GDP in developed countries are closely linked to high per capita energy consumption. As shown by the purchasing power parity (PPP)-based calculation in the World Bank's "World Development Report (1999)," countries with high levels of per capita income also have high per capita energy consumption. In 1999, Japan's per capita energy consumption was 4.96 times larger than China's and its GDP was seven times bigger; US per capita energy consumption and GDP were 9.4 times and 8.8 times larger than China's, respectively; in developed European countries, per capita energy consumption and GDP were four to seven times and five to seven times larger, respectively.[14] In the same year, per capita primary energy consumption in Japan, the US, and the OECD countries was at 5.8 tons, 11.6 tons and 6.7 tons of standard coal equivalent, respectively, while China's was only about 1 ton of standard coal equivalent.[15] Therefore, China's total energy demand will climb to 7.5 billion tons of standard coal equivalent by 2050 when the population is projected to top 1.5 billion and per capita energy consumption will be 5 tons of standard coal equivalent (around 75% of the level of OECD countries in 1999). This will be 5.8 times the amount in 2000 (1.3 billion tons of standard coal equivalent). This gigantic number will have a disruptive impact on global energy politics and the ecological environment.

According to the International Energy Agency:

> *A level of per-capita income in China and India comparable with that of the industrialised countries would, on today's model, require a level of*

[14]Ji Baoping, "Jingji Zengzhang Yu Nengyuan Xiaofei De Guanxi [The Relation between Economic Growth and Energy Consumption]." Available at http://www.bjpopss.gov.cn/bjpssweb/n8874c52.aspx.

[15]See Deng Yingtao, "Xin Nengyuan Geming yu Fazhan Fangshi Yueqian [New Energy Revolution and Transition of Developmental Mode]," Shanghai People's Press, 2013, pp. 33–34; Japan Energy Conservation Handbook, 2008.

energy use beyond the world's energy resource endowment and the absorptive capacity of the planet's ecosystem.

Thus, the IEA expects that:

All countries — China, India, the industrialised countries and the rest of the global community — co-operate on moving quickly towards a genuinely sustainable lifestyle.[16]

Thus, the future of China's sustainable growth rests on a shift toward a sustainable energy structure. China's current over-reliance on traditional fossil fuels, such as coal and oil, in its energy consumption structure is difficult to sustain. Diversification is the only way ahead and should include development of renewable energy and new types of traditional energy and technologies as well as promotion of power-saving technologies and continuous improvement in energy efficiency.

(1) *Renewable Energy Development*

Renewable energy has a special appeal because it is environmentally-friendly. It is generally believed that renewable energy over the next 100 years or so will refer to reliance on solar rays to generate electricity (and not include geothermal power). In fact, it can be roughly divided into the following categories:

Hydropower— using falling water to drive turbines that generate electricity. China's exploitable hydroelectric potential is estimated at 542 million kilowatts based on domestic technologies.[17]

Wind power — wind farms utilizing wind turbines. China's onshore and shallow sea wind power potential is estimated at more than 1 billion kilowatts.[18]

---

[16] IEA: "World Energy Outlook 2007."

[17] The Information Office of the State Council: "China's Energy Policy 2012," White Paper, October, 2012.

[18] He Zuoxiu and Wang Yinan, "Fengli Fadian — Woguo Nengyuan he Dianli Kechixu Fazhan Zhanlue de Zuixianshi Xuanze [Wind Power — the Most Realistic

Biomass — using plant materials and animal manure as fuels to generate electricity. In China, crop straw, woodland waste and marginal plants together can provide about 4 billion tons of biomass, which can be converted to about 2.667 billion tons of coal equivalent at a conversion ratio 1.5:1.[19]

Solar power — includes concentrated solar power, which uses photovoltaic cells and large concentrating lens to generate electricity by concentrating solar rays, and distributed solar power generation, such as green buildings and rooftop solar water heaters.

If the batteries used in electric-powered vehicles were charged using any of the above renewable sources, they would also be regarded as a type of renewable energy.

The potential of renewable energy in China is massive. Developing and utilizing these renewable resources will involve technology and cost. On the technology front, technical issues related to the utilization of hydropower, wind power and distributed solar energy have basically been resolved. And while final breakthroughs are awaited for some technologies (for example, concentrated solar power), the rapid pace of advance should ensure that it will not take long to overcome current technological barriers or improve existing technologies, provided there are sufficient funds. In addition to technology, it will also involve large-scale construction projects such as the building of power plants as well as power storage, transmission and transformer equipment and facilities. And in the end, there is still the problem of funding.

On the cost front, power produced by renewable energy is more expensive than that by traditional coal-fired plants. However, if we add the environmental toll caused by coal-fired plants to its overall cost, then the cost comparison between renewable energy power generation and coal-fired generation will probably change.

Choice for China's Sustainable Development of Energy and Power]," Study on Dialectics of Nature/Ziran Bianzhengfa Yanjiu, 2004, October Issue.

[19] For more data on biomass, see Deng Yingtao, "Xin Nengyuan Geming yu Fazhan Fangshi Yueqian [New Energy Revolution and Transition of Developmental Mode]," Shanghai People's Press, 2013, pp. 7–8 for data related to biomass energy.

Meanwhile, there is plenty of room to reduce the cost of renewable energy by improving technology and in particular by ramping up scale. Most importantly is the fact that renewable energy is inexhaustible and does not produce any environmental pollution and therefore, should be among the core projects to achieve the national goal of developing sustainable energy.

(2) *New Development of Traditional Energy*

Over the years, prophetic predictions about the depletion of traditional energy sources, especially oil, have swirled around ceaselessly. The rise of China, India and other large emerging economies add more uncertainties to world oil supply and demand. However, Daniel Yergin, a leading international energy expert, pointed out after examining a variety of data and actual facts that oil and other traditional fossil fuels will continue to serve as the main source of energy for a long time to come. First, the pace of discovery of new oil fields is slowing, but advances in exploration technologies, especially development in marine exploration, continue to expand and improve the level of oil extraction.[20] Second, new reserves are constantly being

[20]Driven by growing global energy demand, technological advances enable people to exploit untouched regions and energies. Unconventional energies have made unprecedented development, with deepwater production becoming especially active, making it a new battleground in the world oil industry. At the end of 2009, global offshore exploration and production wells numbered about 14,000. Deepwater oil production surged from 1.5 million barrels/day in 2000 to 5 million barrels/day in 2009. Some of the areas with the greatest prospects were at the corners of what is called the Golden Triangle — the waters off Brazil and West Africa and the Gulf of Mexico. By 2009, the shallow and deep waters of the Gulf of Mexico together were accounting for 30% of US domestic oil production. That year, for the first time since 1991, US oil production increased instead of declining, and the deepwater area was the largest single source of growth. The world's proven oil reserves at the end of 2011 reached 1.65 trillion barrels, surpassing the level at the beginning of 2009. Based on an analysis using a database that includes 70,000 oil fields and 4.7 million individual wells, there is no proof that the world is running out of oil. Global oil reserves keep growing. Based on the analysis of the current situation, it will take many years before oil output reaches a plateau. See Daniel Yergin, "Nengyuan Chongsu Shijie [The Quest: Energy, Security, and the Remaking

discovered in developed oil fields in the process of extraction.[21] Third, thanks to the rising oil price, a lot of undeveloped oil and gas resources are now being developed. Development of some unconventional oil and gas resources also has made major breakthroughs. For example, oil beneath the pre-salt layer under the seabed along the Brazilian coastline, Canada's massive oil sands, and the Orinoco heavy oil belt in Venezuela. In terms of form, oil has appeared in more and more varieties. It is estimated that by 2030, unconventional oil will account for one-third of world's total production capacity.[22]

---

of the Modern World]," Trans. Zhu Yuben, Yan Zhimin, Petroleum Industry Press, Beijing, China, 2012, p. 210.

[21] A crucial point on oil production is highlighted by Daniel Yergin in his book, "The Quest: Energy, Security, and the Remaking of the Modern World" (Penguin Press, 2011): "Most of the world's supply is not the result of discoveries, but of reserves and additions. When a field is first discovered, very little is known about it, and initial estimates are limited and generally conservative. As the field is developed, better knowledge emerges about its reserves and production. More wells are drilled, and with better knowledge, proven reserves are very often increased." Taking the US as an example: a study by the United States Geological Survey showed that "86% of oil reserves in the United States are the result not of what is estimated at time of discovery but of the revisions and additions that come with further development." (Chinese edition: "Nengyuan Chongsu Shijie," Trans. Zhu Yuben and Yan Zhimin, Petroleum Industry Press, Beijing, China, 2012, p. 210.

[22] Exploration and development of pre-salt areas in Brazil and oil sands in Canada have produced desirable results.

Pre-salt area in Brazil: The Santos basin stretches 800 miles, running parallel to the southern coastline of Brazil. Below the seabed is the salt deposit at an average depth of more than one mile. Initial exploration shows that the pre-salt layer contains rich oil resources. The first successful oil well was sunk in 6,000 ft of water and drilled to a depth of 15,000 ft under the seabed. The estimated 5 billion to 8 billion barrels of recoverable oil prompted the country's president at the time, Luiz Inácio Lula da Silva, to call the field "the second independence for Brazil." Brazil's incumbent president, Dilma Rousseff has called the oil a "passport to the future."

Oil sands in Canada: Made of viscous bitumen seeped into the sand, oil sands are usually in a solid state, while in warm weather, small amounts of viscous bitumen seeps out of the ground. Oil sands are mainly located in frigid areas in Canada, making bitumen too hard to pump. Not until the late 1990s did oil sands become a large-scale commercial resource, thanks to technological advances and government

What is particularly worth mentioning is the shale gas revolution in the US. Shale gas was first extracted as a resource in Fredonia, New York, in 1821, in shallow, low-pressure fractures. However, due to technical and cost difficulties, shale gas was not economically viable for a long time. In the early 2000s, US-based Devon Energy Corporation started the shale gas revolution after combining fracking and horizontal drilling. The estimated reserves of natural gas in North America have now reached 3,000 trillion cubic feet, which is enough to meet demand for at least 100 years. In 2000, shale gas production accounted for only 1% of natural gas production in the US By 2011, this proportion had increased to 25%. In the next 20 years, this is expected to reach 50%.[23] The tremendous development of shale gas in North America coincided with great progress in liquefied natural gas (LNG). In 2011, Qatar's LNG production capacity reached 77 million tons, accounting for 28% of global production. Global LNG production continues to set record highs.

As natural gas is relatively low-carbon and environment-friendly, it is already playing a role in power generation. In terms of renewable power generation, natural gas is an effective and

---

promotion efforts in taxes and regulation. Since 1997, a total of US$120 billion has been spent on Alberta's oil sands projects, whose output soared from 500,000 barrels per day in 2000 to 1.7 million barrels per day in 2002. It is estimated that the figure could rise to 3 million barrels per day by 2020, higher than the current oil production of Venezuela and Kuwait. If including conventional oil, Canada's oil production in 2029 will reach nearly 4 million barrels per day. Oil sands have made Canada become the world's fifth-largest country by oil production and the world's second largest by oil reserves. Proven oil reserves have increased from 5 billion barrels to 180 billion barrels.

[23] Currently, the main issues with US shale gas are related to environment and policy. One focus is on water pollution, as the chemicals used in the fracking process may contaminate the groundwater resources. Another issue is the problem of backflow, which refers to the handling, regulation and safety emission of the "output liquid," a result of fracking that flows back to the ground. Daniel Yergin, "Nengyuan Chongsu Shijie [The Quest: Energy, Security, and the Remaking of the Modern World]," Trans. Zhu Yuben and Yan Zhimin, Petroleum Industry Press, Beijing, China, 2012, p. 303. (The English-version is "The Quest: Energy, Security, and the Remaking of the Modern World," Penguin Press, 2011).

necessary supplemental fuel. In short, advances in technology, including development in conventional drilling technology, improvement in supply efficiency via long-distance pipelines, and expansion of LNG businesses, the global use of natural gas is expected to continue to grow. And because the US natural gas market has achieved self-sufficiency, it has forced producers to seek new markets for their large volumes of natural gas in Asia.

(3) *New Energy Development Based on New Technological Breakthroughs*

In addition to all the potential energy development mentioned above, advances in science and technology are driving the new energy revolution. In fact, from the eras of firewood to coal and then to petroleum, human society has experienced great transformations, both economically and socially, marked by changes in primary energy. These transformations themselves are the outcome of the energy challenges of the time. Today, the increasingly serious global energy situation will inevitably spawn a new era of the energy revolution. According to Cai Jinshui's research, there are signs indicating that the world is at the brink of a new technological revolution and that "the world is facing a revolutionary breakthrough in new energy."[24]

A new transformation in the concept of matter is the foundation for an energy technology revolution. Mankind has already started to overturn his old views of matter and energy. New energies in nature that were previously undiscovered or were unable to be utilized at the time have been ceaselessly unearthed and put into use.

Vacuum zero-point energy — according to modern science, a vacuum is not a space devoid of matter, but a system composed of positive and negative electronic spinning waves. It is full of flickering particles with the energy field rising and falling above the zero point. The accompanying energy is the zero-point energy or

---

[24] Cai Jinshui, "Renlei de Shuguang — Shijie Nengyuan Zhengmianling Gemingxing de Tupo," Caiyue Wengao, 2013, No. 5. Content in this paragraph is mainly from this article.

vacuum energy. The main current research and applications are in vacuum-energy and proton-energy engines, vacuum-energy generators and tesla coil, among others. Breakthroughs in any of these areas will open immeasurable room for utilization. Both China and the US have poured funds into research and development of these technologies.

Magnetic Energy — the earth is a large magnetic field and existing generators create electric current by cutting magnetic lines with metal particles. Thus, scientifically speaking, it can be imagined that by using a huge plate made of metal wires to cut the magnetic field of the earth, it could generate enough electricity to meet the needs of mankind. At the application level, a neodymium magnet (NdFeB), the so-called "`king of magnets" — a 1 kg NdFeB permanent magnet has been used to pull 4 tons of iron — offers the possibility of using magnetic energy to power engines. According to media reports, the Ministry of Science and Technology of China plans to develop a new type of traction drive system based on a permanent magnet motor. The permanent magnet traction motor system, built by China South Locomotive & Rolling Stock Corporation Limited and already in commercial use in electric vehicles, has run over 7,000 km in testing for a metro system.[25]

Technological breakthroughs in nuclear energy — even though nuclear power is economical, the existing nuclear fission technology uses uranium as the raw material, which not only emits powerful nuclear radiation that is harmful to the human body, but also requires complex methods of disposal. A series of nuclear accidents like Three Mile Island in the US in 1979, the Chernobyl disaster in Ukraine in 1986 and the Fukushima Daiichi nuclear disaster in Japan in 2011 have all exposed the enormous risks of existing nuclear technology, casting a shadow over the use of nuclear energy.

[25] Zhong Yuwei and Liu Chunrui, "Gaosulieche Jiang Jixu Tigaosudu," *The Beijing News*, April 19, 2012.

However, efforts by the scientific community are driving breakthroughs in safe and reliable new nuclear technologies. In the US, Bill Gates, the founder of Microsoft, voiced his support of "traveling wave reactor" technology, which can constrain the diffusion and action of the core fuel to alter the fission reaction, so that the spent nuclear fuel can be reprocessed into a usable fuel after combustion and then burned up completely. That is to say, the uranium isotopes that currently can only be discarded or simply converted into nuclear waste can instead be completely burned out to generate energy in a "traveling wave reactor." Therefore, except for the enriched uranium required at the beginning, a "traveling wave reactor" will need no refueling and create no nuclear waste, making nuclear power a safe, reliable and formidable energy source.

In China, in addition to the significant progress made in "fast reactor" technology, which is similar to a "traveling wave reactor," more commitment has been made to the development of thorium-based reactors, which are safer, cleaner and more economical.[26] China has a large reserve of thorium, which can be easily refined and will not produce carbon dioxide. For thorium-based power stations, there is no need to worry about a meltdown of the reactor core and during the process of power generation, the radioactive substances are only 0.6% of that used by existing nuclear power plants. If "traveling wave reactors" or thorium-based nuclear power plants can be built and widely utilized, the energy structure of mankind will be fundamentally altered.

Scientists are also actively developing and making breakthroughs in other cutting-edge and future technologies, such as

[26] Professor Li Jiayang, Vice President of Chinese Academy of Sciences at the time, said that currently, the proven uranium deposits in China are limited. The Chinese Academy of Sciences is focusing on how to use thorium to fuel fission nuclear reactors, which will help China solve the supply bottleneck in raw materials for nuclear power. In January 2011, the Chinese Academy of Sciences announced that China has initiated a plan to spend 20 years developing nuclear power systems using thorium molten salt reactors.

See Chen He'neng, "Du Yuan Su: Heneng Kaifa Xinsilu," *Beijing Daily*, June 29, 2011.

thermonuclear fusion, cold nuclear fission, hydrogen reactor and quantum teleportation. In short, the universe is full of all kinds of energy, but most of them cannot be utilized due to the current level of technological development. However, humankind can tap nature for endless energy with new technological breakthroughs.

(4) *Development of Distributed Energy Systems and Smart Grids*

So-called distributed energy changes the traditional energy economic model of centralized production, centralized processing and distributed consumption into a format whereby the flat distribution of solar and wind power, biomass and other renewable energies on the planet can be systematically linked via the dispersed construction of electrical and heat sources with a smart grid. Promotion of distributed energy will be focused on the distributed generation, which will enable every building and every family in every city of every country to receive energy from the surrounding natural environment. Compared to large centralized power generation units, distributed generation facilities merge multiple small-and-medium-sized power sources to make up the total generation capacity. Compared with the small independent power producers of the past, capacity allocation and layout of distributed generation facilities will conform to a regular pattern to meet overall requirements, so that once difficult problems like connecting dispersed power sources to the network and utilization can be solved.

Among the various kinds of distributed generation, the prospect of distributed solar energy looks particularly promising. Photovoltaic power generation is mobile, independent and small. It makes use of roofs (new materials can also be used on exterior walls), which means it does not take up space on the ground and also has no transmission losses as the power used inside the house is generated from the top of the building. In addition, it can provide *round-the-clock power*, reducing the pressure during peak hours.

Use of distributed energy will have the most potential in China's rural areas, which have the following characteristics: (1) large in scale — rural areas account for 43% of total national energy consumption;

(2) household energy consumption accounts for a large portion; (3) biomass is the major source of energy. It is estimated that about 220 million tons of straw and 50 million cubic meters of firewood are burnt annually nationwide.[27]

Smart grid technology is the precondition that makes the distributed energy system possible. It allows every household to generate electricity and feed that power into the grid instead of using it themselves, so as to avoid the difficulties of power storage. *As described by Jeremy Rifkin,* people can use:

> *...Internet technology to transform the power grid of every continent into an energy internet that acts just like the Internet (when millions of buildings are generating a small amount of renewable energy locally, on-site, they can sell surplus green electricity back to the grid and share it with their continental neighbours).*[28]

(2) *Water, Land and Other Resources*

China is short of water, with the per capita amount at 2,100 cubic meters, which is only 28% of the world average.[29] Of the 2.8 trillion cubic meters of water resources in China, every year, 730 billion cubic meters flow out over the nation's border or into rivers shared by China and its neighboring countries.[30] But in actual fact, China is not completely out of water, but lacks the capability to fully utilize the water

---

[27] Zeng Jing and Zhang Weibing, "Woguo Nongcun Nengyuan Weiti Yanjiu," *Journal of Guizhou University* (Social Science Edition), 2005, No. 5.

[28] Jeremy Rifkin, "Disanci Gongye Geming — Xinjingji Moshi Ruhe Gaibian Shijie [The Third Industrial Revolution: How Lateral Power is Transforming Energy, the Economy, and the World], Trans. Zhang Tiwei and Sun Yuning, CITIC Press, 2012. (English version: "The Third Industrial Revolution: How Lateral Power is Transforming Energy, the Economy, and the World," Palgrave MacMillan, 2011).

[29] Li Guoying's speech on water and food security in a branch meeting of the Yellow River Forum on September 26, 2012. Available at: http://www.mwr.gov.cn/ztpd/2012ztbd/dwjhhgjlt/ldjh/201209/t 20120927_329961.html.

[30] Jiao Yong's speech at the Press Conference held by the Press Office of the State Council on the current water situation and 12th Five-Year Water Plan on October 12, 2011. Available at: http://www.mwr.gov.cn/hdpt/zxft/zxzb/slxs.

resources it does have. In the western regions, there is more water but fewer people with great volumes of water flowing uselessly out into the Indian Ocean; in eastern regions, there are more people but less water. Even the "South–North Water Diversion Project" cannot solve the overall scarcity of water in the region. A fundamental solution would be to begin a "West–East Water Diversion Project," transferring water from the Yarlung Tsangpo River and the Three Parallel Rivers to the Yangtze and Yellow Rivers in the east. This major proposal is called the "Shuotian Project." Previously, the project faced significant technological and ecological obstacles, such as the difficulties in constructing large-scale power plants required for the diversion and pumping projects in the Hengduan Mountains. Other problems involved water transmission conduits needed in the first stages of the "South–North Water Diversion" in the western regions.[31] However, these technical problems have basically been solved with the major advances of recent years in wind power technology and tunnel engineering. The remaining problem is funding: this project will require an astronomical investment over an extremely long period. However, it is related to the nation's long-term fortunes with far-reaching significance.

China is not short of land. The problem is that the amount of usable land as a proportion of the nation's total area is too small. Currently, the state has set 1.8 billion mu of arable land as the bare minimum, which is an absolute necessity.[31] As a nation that will need to feed 1.5 billion people in the future, China cannot count on the international grain market to solve its food problems. Therefore, as the yield per unit of land has reached a high level and further significant increases would be difficult, the current scale of arable land must be maintained.[32] However, urbanization is also a goal of China's sustainable development. As mentioned earlier, in

[31] Guo Kai *et al.*, "Sutian Yunhe — Nanshui Beidiao Gongcheng," *China Statistics*, 1999, No. 2.

[32] The 12th Five-Year Plan for National Economic and Social Development of the People's Republic China, endorsed in the Fourth Session of the 10th National People's Congress in 2006, clearly stated that 1.8 billion mu of farmland is set as an

the next two to three decades, 300 million to 400 million rural residents will migrate to urban areas. Therefore, it is inevitable that tens of millions of acres of land will be transformed from rural to urban use.

How to improve urban land utilization ratio is a policy issue worth exploring. As urbanization is designed to improve the quality of people's lives and living standards, we should avoid approaches adopted by Hong Kong and Singapore, where a large portion of the population is concentrated in densely located, ultra-high buildings. Instead, as much as possible, we should consider building "green towns" and people-friendly factories, providing an appropriate space and environment in which to live and work.[33] Against this backdrop, the only way to ensure the two strategic objectives of self-sufficiency in food security and people-oriented urbanization is to increase the supply of *usable land.* Currently, the central government insists on a principle of balancing land use with replenishment of arable land. That is, however much arable land has been used for urbanization, an identical amount of new arable land must be added elsewhere. From a long-term perspective, this principle should be further extended to incorporate a forward-looking and integrated effective land growth strategy so as to scientifically and systematically increase the supply of usable land.

There are two aspects to this so-called "increasing the supply of usable land": The first is "reclamation," which refers to converting deserts, barren hills and wastelands into land suitable for afforestation, cultivation or living on after comprehensive improvement work. For this kind of "reclamation," there are no fundamental technological problems. The most critical issue is capital. The second is "amelioration," which refers to improving the quality and yield of the land already in use. Currently, only a small portion of China's agricultural land could be considered high-standard farmland.

---

obligatory target with legal effect and a bottomline that cannot be crossed. (See website of Ministry of Land and Resources of China).

[33] China's grain production reached 331.5 kg per mu in 2010. Available at: http://www.stats.gov.cn/tjfx/grgd/t20110301_402706373.htm.

If all existing agricultural land infrastructure is to be upgraded to high standards, it will require unified planning of land division, irrigation, water conservancy and windbreaks, and even irrigation technology. Implementation must be backed by continuous investment of capital and labor, which may, in turn, negate the need for the government-set minimum of 1.8 billion mu of arable land to secure national food security.[34]

Another related issue is how to improve the utilization of woodlands, grasslands and maritime areas. The woodland and grassland areas are each about twice the size of China's arable land,[35] but the current utilization and yield ratios are still low. In recent years, through programs to "return the farmlands to forests and pastures" and the constant deepening of reforms to the system of collective forest rights, society's enthusiasm for afforestation has been mobilized, speeding the flow of various factors of production into the forestry industry. The potential of the woodlands, its species, the market and workforce has been fully unleashed. As of 2011, 178 million hectares of forest land, or 97.8% of the collective forest rights,[36] have been contracted to farmers. By improving technologies, increasing investment and enhancing the level of management, the yield ratio of woodlands and grasslands will be raised continuously

[34]According to 2011 census data published on the China Hong Kong SAR government website, the population density is 6,544 people/km^2. Population density of Hong Kong Island and Kowloon are 15,924 people/km^2 and 44,917 people/km^2, respectively. According to the 2010 census data published on the Singaporean government website, Singapore's population density is about 5,270 people/km^2.

[35]On March 16, 2012, the State Council of China approved the National Land Remediation Plan 2011–2015. The 12th Five-Year Plan period regarding land reclamation proposed establishing another 400 million mu of basic farmland with high standards, ensuring stable yields regardless of drought or excessive rain; add an additional 24 million mu farmland; to improve 4.5 million mu land which are dispersed, abandoned, idle and inefficient; to rehabilitate damaged land and attain a reclamation rate of more than 35%. See Mao Zhi Hong and Yang Lei, "2012 Gengdi Baohu Liangdian Fengcheng," *Territory Resource News*, January 18, 2013.

[36]China's arable land covers 1,217,200 km^2, forests 2,360,900 km^2 and pasture 2,618,400 km^2. National Bureau of Statistics of China, "China Statistical Yearbook 2012," China Statistical Publishing House, 2012.

and effectively and the under-forest economy, which mainly involves planting, cultivating, harvesting and processing related products and utilizing forestry landscape, will be developed vigorously and to a certain extent achieve an alternative to the traditional products of the land.

Whether it is "reclamation," "amelioration" or the utilization of woodland, grassland and other resources, there are not any fundamental technological barriers to carrying out these programs. As long as the funding is stable over the long-term, China's usable land area can be increased gradually, which is the fundamental way to solve the land problem.

For other resources, including non-ferrous metals, ferrous metals, organic substances and inorganic substances, China may or may not have plentiful reserves. Among them, reserves of tungsten and rare earth are relatively abundant, while per capita resources of iron, copper, aluminum and other metals are significantly lower than the world average. However, as commodities are basically available in the trading network of the global market, most resource issues eventually come down to an issue of money. It should be noted that as demand for such commodities from China, India and other large emerging economies will remain strong for a long time into the future, prices of these materials should continue on an upward trend for some time yet. But as commodities are also traded as financial futures and their prices may be manipulated by financial oligarchs seeking profits, they are not in a conventional market economy characterized by free competition. Thus, securing the security of China's strategic commodities is not merely an issue of funding, but also how to effectively use the funds. Special management of an organic combination of equity investment, directional lending, hedging, trade in goods and other means of asset management should be explored.

In short, energy, resources, water and land issues appear beset with difficulties, but fundamentally speaking, all these are problems and they come back to funding: how will they be financed and who will invest?

5. Human Capital and Technological Innovation

(1) *Human Capital*

The disappearance of "the demographic dividend" is a major cause for concern in regards to the prospects for China's long-term growth.[37] The so-called "demographic dividend" in the past referred to the simple large labor force and their low wages. This "dividend" will eventually disappear in line with the gradual decline of the surplus rural population and as the goals of economic growth puts value in "people-first." We should not hope to build the nation's economic growth on the low incomes of the majority of the working population.

However, the disappearance of the "demographic dividend" that is based on the surplus rural population does not mean the disappearance of the dividend related to human capital. Consumption and industrial upgrades will become the theme for industrial changes in China's new stage of development. Thus, there will no longer be the urgent need for the simple labor force that is sourced directly from among the rural workers. Instead, it will be a highly-trained, high-quality, skilled and professional work force that is in great demand. From the development of the strategic emerging industries, the transformation of traditional industries, to the long-term growth of high-end consumer and service industries, demand for professional and skilled workers will be huge. Therefore, the old low-level, simple demographic dividend will disappear, while the new higher-level, skilled demographic dividend awaits development.

---

[37] Over the past 10 years, afforestation in China has covered 863 million mu in total, which is the largest ever afforestation area in a 10-year period, increasing nearly 100 million mu compared with the previous 10 years. During the past 10 years, despite the continued decline in global forest resources, China achieved growth both in forest area and forest stock volume. National forest area increased from 2.39 billion mu to 2.93 billion mu, forest stock from 11.3 billion cubic meters to 13.7 billion cubic meters. Xinhuanet, "10nian Zaolin 8.63yi Mu Guotu Luhua Bufa Quanmian Jiakuai," June 16, 2012.

The key is to build a sound and prudent vocational training system and securing the capital investment that will be required.

(2) *Technological Innovation*

Some people believe that China's rapid economic growth has come at the cost of high input and low efficiency. Some even assert that China's economic growth did not produce any significant technological progress. In fact, since the reform and opening up, China's economy not only has achieved supernormal growth in the aggregate, but also constantly advanced the transition of the industrial structure and labor productivity. Today, most products in China's national economy did not even exist before reform and opening up, such as information technology electronics, the Internet and the high-speed rail. Even industries that existed before reform and opening up, such as the steel, cement and automobile sectors, have made great progress in terms of scale, technology and efficiency. In the high-tech fields, China has not only accomplished the launch of a manned spacecraft — "Shenzhou"[38] — and the deepwater submarine "Jiaolong,"[39] sent the lunar probe "Chang'e 2" to pass close

[38] There have been doubts raised about the "demographic dividend" in the academic community. For example, Professor Chen Dongqi (2008), based on his study of China's statistical data, believes that it still cannot be determined whether the demographic dividend was the key driver of economic growth, even when considering the whole process since reform and opening up. The real driving force behind growth in the past 30 years is the continuous improvement in productivity fostered by institutional innovation, technological progress and human capital. See Chen Dongqi, "Jingji Zengzhang Yu Laodong Shengchanlv — Tanxun Gaige Sanshinian Jingji Gaosu Zengzhang De Yuanyin," reprinted from "Zhongguo Jingji Wushiren Kan Sanshinian — Huigu Yu Fengxi," Ed. by Wu Jinglian *et al.*, China Economic Press, 2008.

[39] After the successful launch of the first manned spacecraft, Shenzhou 5, in 2003, China launched successive manned spacecrafts: Shenzhou 6 and Shenzhou 7, and the unmanned Shenzhou 8. On June 16, 2012, Shenzhou 9 was launched. On June 18, Shenzhou 9 docked with the Tiangong 1 space station. On June 29, Shenzhou 9 returned to Earth. It demonstrates that China is proficient in automatic docking technology and manned space technology. Shenzhou 9 was China's longest space flight.

to the asteroid Tutadisi,[40] and delivered the nation's first aircraft carrier "Liaoning,"[41] but also become an exporter of high-speed rail technology.

Of course, there are still substantial gaps between China and the developed countries, whether they be in cutting-edge scientific fields or in terms of the overall level of technological advancement in the main sectors. For example, China does not lack domestic vehicle brands, but most are low-end cars and there are basically no high-end brands like BMW and Audi; China is a major manufacturer of engineering machinery, but it is still reliant on foreign countries to supply the large engines and even the hydraulic systems that go in them; China's annual residential construction area ranks as the largest in the world and the scale of the building materials industry is also very big, but the high-end residential glass and flooring materials still need to be imported or supplied by joint ventures; supply of elevators is largely dependent on foreign-owned companies; China is a major global consumer and manufacturer in terms of microelectronics, but it still relies on imports for the supply of the core chips. Precisely, because of these reasons, the central government has set out the strategic task to build an innovation-oriented country and vigorously promoted the development of the strategic emerging industries. It is worth noting that in order to build a nation of innovators, China cannot just focus on catching up with or making breakthroughs in the global cutting-edge technologies. In the coming decades, there will be more frequent and widespread challenges for China in product upgrades in the main industrial sectors and research and development in related applications.

---

[40] On June 27, 2012, the manned submarine Jiaolong reached a depth of 7,062 m, marking a breakthrough in China's deep-diving technology.

[41] On December 13, 2012, China's lunar probe Chang'e 2, traveled about 7 million kilometers from Earth to make a successful pass of Tutadisi, an asteroid named after the "God of War" in Western mythology. The relative distance between Chang'e 2 and Tutadisi was controlled at around 15 km, at relative speed of nearly 11 km/s. Chang'e 2 took close-up images of Tutadisi, achieving the goal of its mission to "accurately measure the track, accurately control the satellite and accurately shoot the image." By now, Chang'e 2 has flown 20 million kilometers from the Earth.

As mentioned above, China is now able to manufacture most of the technology-intensive products available in the world today. The problem is that there are real gaps in product grades, inherent quality and even the cultural tastes reflected by the products. These gaps cannot be eliminated through disjointed, one-off major breakthroughs, but instead by sustained, broad, solid and cumulative improvements. From processing methods, technology, to operators' skills, experience and product testing and marketing, continuous improvements will be required for all aspects of the entire value chain. Moreover, this kind of continuous improvement requires related industries to develop simultaneously. That is to say, to accomplish the technological and industrial upgrades of the main industrial sectors, a vigorous and application-oriented research and development system for technology and management will be required, covering the main sectors of the national economy. There are no insurmountable barriers, but it urgently requires the support of national-level investment and long-term promotion.

6. National Defense Construction

China's supernormal growth since the reform and opening up is also an outcome of the nation's adherence to a peaceful development strategy. Since Deng Xiaoping promulgated this strategy, China has been afforded the rare opportunity of decades of international peace — provided by the globalization process — to put economic construction front and center, making full use of both international and domestic markets and resources to achieve great unconventional leaps in development. However, the global strategic situation has undergone profound changes since the beginning of the 21st century. As China has grown into the world's second-largest economy, its development strategy and industrial policy will greatly affect the global economy situation. Therefore, changes in the global economy, especially in the financial industry and strategic resources, will always affect China's economic development.

China's goal is peaceful development; however, the lessons of history and the logic of reality tell us: a nation can only seek peace when it dares to fight; lasting peace requires strong national defense. Poverty and backwardness may not necessarily be overcome, but a rich nation that is also frail will certainly not escape the misfortune of being bullied.[42] Therefore, the balance of power between the major nations is a necessary condition to keep the peace. There have been many painful lessons in Chinese history whereby thriving internal development was abruptly interrupted by external violence. During the Song Dynasty, the economy and culture were flourishing,[43] but the Jin invasion ended the Northern Song regime; Mongolian cavalry overthrew the Southern Song regime after the Song Dynasty retreated to south of the Yangtze River. In the late Qing Dynasty, the Self-strengthening Movement was the prelude to China's modern reforms, but the First Sino-Japanese War heralded the bankruptcy of the movement and eventually led to the downfall of the Qing Dynasty. In the 1920s and 1930s, Chinese national capital had developed rapidly as Western countries were busy with their own affairs. But "The Marco Polo Bridge Incident" once again brutally interrupted the process of China's national economic development and pushed the nation into years of war and misery.

Therefore, to sustain peaceful development, China must have a strong sense of urgency in building a defense force capable of safeguarding national independence and territorial integrity and preventing the nation's sovereignty from being infringed upon.

As an added bonus, breakthroughs in defense science and technology made during the process of this construction are also important driving forces for the nation's overall scientific and technological progress. After the Second World War, the US and other developed capitalist countries ushered in the golden age of economic development, which to a large extent benefited from converting cutting-edge military technologies to civilian use. For a very long time, many people believed that the collapse of the Soviet

---

[42] On September 25, 2012, the aircraft carrier "Liaoning" was commissioned into the People's Liberation Army Navy.

[43] Zhu Weizhen, "Aida Biying Luohou?" reprinted from "Chongdu Jindaishi" Zhongxi Book Company, 2010.

Union was because of an overemphasis on the defense industry, causing the entire national economy to be dragged down. This view is very one-sided. Historically, the US defense budget has risen for decades. In 2011, the US defense budget was over US$700 billion. But the defense spending system in the US is different from that in the former Soviet Union. It adopts an open system that incorporates both military and civilian instead of an absolute separation between the two.[44] Thus, high defense spending has not caused the US economy to slide, but, on the contrary, has provided a boost over a long period.

Therefore, as long as China can rationalize the relationship between the defense and civilian industries and ensure positive interactions, then further increase in national defense construction will not only serve the needs of national security, but also provide impetus for fundamentally improving the nation's technological advancement and industrial capacity.

7. Accumulation, Investment and Consumption

In conclusion, both the internal and external forces that drive China's supernormal growth have undergone significant changes. However, what remains unchanged is that China is still the largest developing nation. Even if the nation turns to an endogenous growth model, there will still be room and foundation for a new round of rapid and stable growth on both the supply and demand sides.

The prevailing view at present is that the macroeconomic imbalance among accumulation, investment and consumption is a major defect in China's economic growth over the past more than 30 years. The phenomenon of the "three lows, three highs" is not merely the

[44] According to Angus Maddison's calculation, when Zhao Kuangyin became emperor in 960 AD, China's population was 55 million and per capita GDP was US$450 (based on the US dollar value in 1990). Both are higher than that seen in the Europe during the same period. See Angus Maddison, "Zhongguo Jingji de Changqi Biaoxian — Gongyuan 960–2030 [Chinese Economic Performance in the Long Run, 960–2030 AD]," Trans. Wu Xiaoying *et al.*, Shanghai People's Publishing House, 2008.

result of the government's development strategies and economic policies, but also a reflection of China's adapting to the objective economic laws during the process of industrialization.

As described in Chapter 1, it is an inherent requirement to increase the per capita fixed capital when a country's economy is shifting from light industry to heavy industry and large-scale urbanization is progressing; an increasingly large part of national output value will become the accumulation of material capital, and a smaller portion will be consumption. Therefore, it is a natural phenomenon that the proportion of consumption to national income tends to decrease in the acceleration phase of a nation's industrialization and urbanization. Additionally, in the early stages of industrialization, China had a large amount of surplus rural labor, which easily satisfied demand for workers. Thus, growth in wage and income levels has been slow for a long time. In fact, the development status of different regions in China also reflects these characteristics. According to Professor Zhang Jun's research, analysis of the statistical data of all provinces and cities shows that the more developed the regions are, the lower the share of consumption in GDP.[46]

---

[45]For a long time, major military powers have consistently paid great attention to integrating national defense and military needs into the overall national strategic development blueprint. From the world-renowned Manhattan Project and Star Wars program, to the Digital Earth strategy, all are defense concepts of preparation for war during peacetime. According to a French study, 85% of core technologies, while also key for civilian applications, can be directly used for military purposes. Currently, over 80% of the US companies that manufacture military supplies are also producing civilian goods. During the Gulf War, in order to protect thousands of troops overseas, more than 80 IT departments in the United States prepared information resources and war materials; 38 airlines, dozens of overseas transport companies and railway authorities of seven states provided transportation support; 73 largescale companies provieded food and medical supplies. During the lraq war, the US military was supported by more than 100,000 information technology professionals in aerospace, shipping, electronics, computers, networks and other fields to facilitate and ensure joint operations. Ouyang Zhao Biao, "Xian Dai Zhan Zheng: Tu Xian Rong He Zhi Sheng Qu Shi," *PLA Daily*, September 22, 2011.

[46]Zhang Jun, "Li Jie Zhong Guo Jing Ji Kuai Su Fa Zhan De Ji Zhi: Zhu Rong Ji Ke Neng Shi Dui De," *Comparative Studies*, Vol. 6, 2012.

Following the same logic, with continuous progress in industrialization, there surely will be a turning point at which the share of consumption in national income will begin to rebound gradually after reaching its lowest point. At this time, the acceleration phase of a nation's per capita fixed capital accumulation will basically come to an end. For China, there is already evidence that in recent years, the share of consumption in national income has begun to rebound. The household consumption ratio curve of the Chinese economy constructed by Professor Li Daokui and his colleagues apparently showed a U-shaped trend reversal around 2007.[47] According to their estimates, the household consumption ratio improved from the lowest point of 35.99% to 47.11% in 2009. It should be noted that the above household consumption ratio did not completely include housing, education, healthcare and other aspects of consumption. Consumption in these areas has been underestimated for a long time. If we have more accurate statistics on housing, healthcare, education and other consumption categories, the household consumption ratio will see larger improvement.[48]

Household disposable income is a relevant indicator of consumption. The ratio of Chinese people's disposable income to GDP is too low, while the foreign trade surplus to GDP ratio is too high. Similar to the situation mentioned above, these two indicators have also begun to improve. As again shown by the research of Professor Li Daokui, the trade surplus to GDP ratio dropped from 8.8% in 2007 to 2.1% in 2011. There are signs showing that China's foreign trade surplus will continue to decline. Meanwhile, imports are rising at a faster pace than that of the decline in exports, indicating that China's domestic demand continues to strengthen.

---

[47] Li Daokui and Xu Xiang, "Shichang Jizhi shi Zhongguo Jingji Jiegou Tiaozheng de Jiben Dongli," *Comparative Studies*, (6), 2012.

[48] US scholars have previously pointed out that China's official statistics underestimate the consumption ratio. See Arvind Subramanian, "Eclipse: Living in the Shadow of China's Economic Dominance," Washington, DC: Peterson Institute for International Economics, 2011.

In short, even without massive government intervention, the strength of the market mechanism will still push the macroeconomic ratios of China's economy toward balance. Considering the sheer size of the Chinese economy, it is impossible to continue to rely on a huge trade surplus to support economic growth and it will inevitably have to rely on domestic demand. However, domestic-driven demand is not the same as consumption-driven. In recent years, China has rolled out more supportive policies on consumption and proposed a vision that during "The 12th Five-Year Plan" period, household income will be doubled and the country will be built into a major global consumer market. All these efforts are necessary. However, using macroeconomic common sense, to increase the consumption levels by artificially adjusting the consumption ratio and therefore stimulating economic growth can only be effective in the short term. In the medium- and long-term, it cannot possibly work,[49] because the products to be consumed first must be produced so that consumption can be increased. Whether expanding the scale of production or increasing productivity, both will be dependent on investment. In the long-term, investment is consumption, which is a necessary condition to increase future consumption.

As can be seen from our analysis in this chapter, China is far from achieving the per capita fixed capital accumulation required to join the ranks of developed countries. Industrialization and urbanization are still in full swing. Taking into account the unique ecological endowments and geopolitical patterns, without prolonged large-scale investment and asset accumulation, it will be impossible for China to achieve social stability and ensure its people can live and work in peace. Therefore, China should accumulate sufficient "baseline" properties to ensure the country's long-term survival and development in areas such as ecological assets, environmental

---

[49] Professor Justin Lin Yifu, and Professor Zhu Tian and Professor Zhang Jun all have pointed out that it is a paradox of economics that economic growth is driven by consumption. Xue Jing: "Lin Yifu: Renhe Shihou Dou Buneng Tichu Yi Xiaofei Ladong Jingji Zengzhang," *China Construction News*, November 9, 2012; Zhu Tian, Zhang Jun: "Bei Wudu De Kai'ensi Lilun," *Economic Observer*, September 24, 2012.

protection, land improvement, human resources, science and technology, urban infrastructure and national defense. Meanwhile, properly handling the relationship among accumulation, investment and consumption is still a significant strategic issue. With the gradual completion of industrialization and urbanization in the decades ahead, it is an inevitable trend that the consumption ratio will rise appropriately and the investment ratio will fall. However, in the long run, we must promote entrepreneurship and doggedly persist with investment and accumulation. At present, China shall not follow the consumer society or welfare society models adopted by the countries of Europe and in America. Even when China joins the ranks of developed countries, we still cannot completely copy the Western models.

Chapter 5

A New Phase for Supernormal Growth

1. The Prospects for Growth Toward 2049

In the 36 years between 2013 and 2049 (not including 2049), what kind of economic growth will China be able to achieve?

First of all, we must look at conventional growth. As discussed in Chapter 1, in the more than 30 years up to today, average annual growth has been over 9%, in which around 7% could be accounted for by the conventional market economic growth segment and the other over 2% resulting from China's special system of supernormal growth. If we were to assume that in the 36 years leading up to 2049, the conventional growth rate in the first 18 years dropped to 6% and in the remaining 18 years, it fell to 4%, conventional economic growth over the entire 36-year period would be average 5% annually. We could say this assumption is not very optimistic.[1]

---

[1] There are many different international statistical estimations of China's future economic expansion, but basically all of them show its long-term economic growth rate will be good. Among those are Professor Barry Eichengreen (2012) who predicts that growth will be 6.1% to 7% between 2012 and 2020 and 5% to 6.2%

Let us look again at the power of supernormal growth. On the supply side, the basic framework has not changed, it is just that the current three-dimensional market system has improved allowing sustained supernormal investment, which has continued to guarantee the support of supernormal growth. From the demand side, while the supernormal international purchasing power driven by the US Federal Reserve no longer exists; however, from our analysis in Chapter 4, we can see that it is not difficult to find endogenous supernormal buying power to provide the extraordinary pull of demand. This allows us to assume that on average every year we could add on about 2 percentage points of supernormal growth. This implies that in the 18 years from 2013 to 2031, the average annual growth rate could be lifted to about 8% and in the following 18 years from 2032 to 2049 to about 6%, with the average rate over the entire 36 years about 7%.

What is the significance of an average growth rate of 7% over 36 years?

(1) *Total GDP Toward 2049*

According to the growth rate mentioned above, what magnitude will China's GDP reach by 2030 and 2049? Table 5.1 and Figure 5.1 show the prospects for growth.

In the table, if we assume that the average annual growth is 7%, China's GDP will reach about RMB570 trillion in 2049 over 36 years. In US dollar terms, that would be US$114 trillion, assuming an exchange rate of 5:1. With a population of 1.5 billion, average per capita GDP would be RMB380,000 or about US$76,000.

---

between 2021 and 2030; Professor Jong-Wha Lee among others estimates that median annual growth will average 6.1% between 2011 and 2030; John S. Wilson (2007), whose estimates were slightly lower at 5.8% between 2008 and 2030; Nobel prize-winning economist Robert Fogel (2007), whose estimates were clearly more optimistic, predicting average annual growth of 8.4% in 2001–2040; and Angus Maddison, whose predictions were more pessimistic, foreseeing growth of only 5% between 2004 and 2030. However, his estimation was more of a personal view and not like those of other researchers whose estimates were based on specific modeling.

Table 5.1 Outlook for China's Economic Growth 2013–2049

Year	Conventional growth (%)	Contribution to growth from supernormal buying power (%)	Supernormal growth (%)	GDP with conventional growth (RMB trillion)	GDP with supernormal growth (RMB trillion)
2013	—	—	—	50.00	50.00
2017	—	—	—	63.12	68.02
2022	6	2	8	84.47	99.95
2027	—	—	—	113.05	146.86
2031	—	—	—	142.72	199.80
2032	—	—	—	148.43	211.79
2037	—	—	—	180.58	283.42
2042	4	2	6	219.71	379.28
2047	—	—	—	267.31	507.56
2049	—	—	—	289.12	570.30

Note: Annual figures are taken from the beginning of the year. For example, the 2013 annual figure is taken from the end value of 2012; 2049's data is taken from the value at the end of 2048, therefore strictly speaking the 36 years do not include 2049.

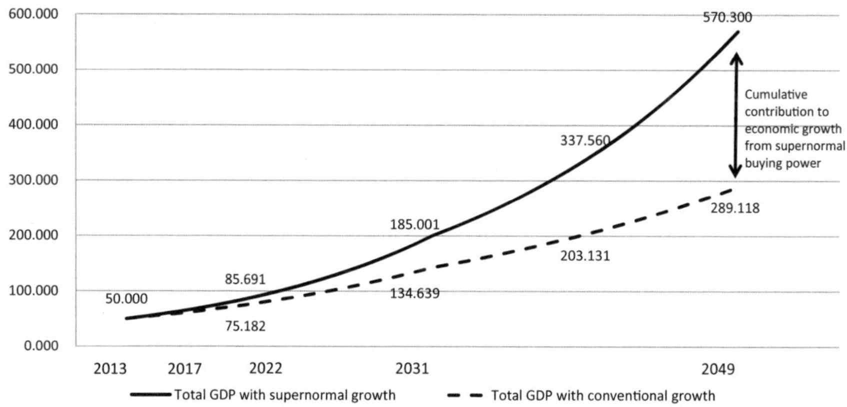

Figure 5.1 Estimates of China's GDP growth 2013–2049.

What does it mean when China's GDP reaches RMB570 trillion or US$114 trillion?

Let us assume that during the same period average annual US economic growth was 2%, with GDP doubling over those 36 years to about US$32 trillion. That is, by 2049 China's GDP will be more than three times larger than that of the US, assuming an exchange rate of 5:1. Of course, as China's population is 1.5 billion compared with 300 million in the US, in terms of per capita GDP, China's is still lower at only about 70% of the US level. It is interesting to note that this simulated prediction is quite consistent with that of Professor Robert Fogel, winner of the Nobel Memorial Prize in Economic Sciences.[2] Fogel estimated that China's average GDP growth between 2000 and 2040 would reach 8.4%, expanding to US$123 trillion, with per capita GDP climbing to US$85,000. He also predicted that the US economy would maintain relatively fast-paced growth (averaging 3.8%), with economic output reaching US$41 trillion and average per capita GDP of US$107,000. Thus, comparing the GDP of China and the US in 2040, China's would be threefold larger with per capita GDP at almost 80% the level in the US.

Additionally, Professor Fogel made itemized predictions about the constraints and risks to the long-term development of the Chinese economy including labor, finance, state-owned enterprises, environment, social stability and political polarization. And even upon this basis, he still confirmed his above estimates.

(2) *Key Macroeconomic Ratios Toward 2049*

First, what level of investment is required to achieve the above-mentioned economic growth rate? Among recent popular neoclassical models of growth, economic expansion has depended upon the factors of production, including capital and labor input,

[2] Robert Fogel, "Capitalism and Democracy in 2040: Forecasts and Speculations," NBER Working Paper, No. 13184, 2007. For more on Fogel's estimates, see Table A.10 in the Appendix.

and technological advancements. Prior to the neoclassical growth model, there was also the comparatively more simple Harrod–Domar model of growth, in which labor input was the derived variable of capital, and economic growth could be estimated just through investment levels and investment efficiency. The final estimates of the two different approaches are the same, with the difference being that the neoclassical growth estimates are more complicated. For simplicity, we will use the old style Harrod–Domar model:

GDP growth rate = investment rate/capital output.

As previously mentioned, the capital–output ratio is the ratio of new investment to incremental GDP, therefore economic growth equals the investment rate divided by the capital–output ratio.

Under this formula, given China's future long-term economic growth rate, to calculate the required investment rate we must first make an estimate of the capital–output ratio. We can predict that compared with the previous several decades, China's capital–output ratio over the next 30 years will decline slightly. The reason for this is that in the past few decades, China has undergone rapid industrialization during which the capital–output ratio has already peaked. In the next several decades as the proportion of tertiary industries increases, the total capital–output ratio should be reduced, or, at the very least, not rise. To facilitate the calculation, we can assume that China's capital–output ratio over the next 36 years basically will not change. According to calculations of overall investment and total GDP growth during related periods, from 1978 to 1994, China's capital–output ratio was 3.5, from 1995 to 2010, it was 4.1 and from 1978 to 2010, the total ratio was almost 4. So let us assume that for the next 36 years it will still be 4.

Looking at international precedents, this assumption has foundation. The US capital–output ratio more or less went through a process of first rising and then stabilizing. If we simply use total investment and total GDP over a 10-year period to calculate, we find that the US capital–output ratio between 1945 and 1954 was

2.5; between 1965 and 1974, it climbed to 3.6; after that it fluctuated between 3.5 and 5 right up until the outbreak of the subprime crisis.[3]

Based on the reasoning that China's capital–output ratio will hold at around 4, we can use the aforementioned economic growth rate to calculate the corresponding investment rate. Over the next 36 years, we can estimate that the growth rate in the first 18 years will be 8%, which, divided by the capital–output ratio means that the investment rate must be 32%; the second 18 years with estimated growth at 6%, correlating to an investment rate of 24%. That is, if the 8% growth of the first 18 years is to be reached, an investment rate of 32% must be maintained; and if a growth rate of 6% is to be achieved over the next 18 years, then an investment rate of 24% must be maintained every year. Currently, China's investment rate is almost 40%, so if we compare that with the previous 30 years, the investment rate over these two periods will clearly drop.

Let us look now at the consumption rate. To do that, we must first make assumptions and estimate what the future trade surplus and government spending will be.

On the trade surplus, it is impossible for China with an economy on such a massive scale to continue to rely on this surplus to achieve economic growth. Currently, China's trade surplus as a proportion of GDP has fallen from 8.77% before the global financial crisis (2007) to 2.61% now (2011). In the future, the surplus may continue to decline, but a comparatively lower proportion of GDP could be sustained, such as 1%. For the convenience of our calculation, we will start from a principle of stability and assume that during a short

[3] These calculations used data from the US Bureau of Economic Analysis. To make an international comparison, we can use data from the International Monetary Fund. According to IMF data, the 10-year total capital–output ratio stabilized around 6, similar to the United Kingdom. Because growth in Japan has stalled the 10-year total capital–output ratio has already reached about 40 in the 21st century. In India, the ratio is almost 4, showing it has made considerable achievement in terms of its industrialization, and its capital–output ratio has increased greatly.

transition period — the next four years for example — China will see imports and exports come into balance with the trade surplus reaching zero by 2017.

Regarding fiscal spending, in 2011 China's fiscal expenditure was RMB10.92 trillion, accounting for 23.1% of GDP. While there is currently no reason to change the ratio of expenditure, for the purposes of our calculation, let us assume it accounts for 20% of GDP. Additionally, of the 2011 fiscal expenditure, RMB6.36 trillion is for consumption, accounting for 13.4% of GDP; government investment is RMB1.48 trillion, or 3% of GDP; the remaining amount is mainly used for transfer payments. We shall assume that these percentage ratios do not change.[4]

Let us look again at the proportion of consumption as part of GDP. With the assumed 2017 trade surplus at zero, the amount of investment as a proportion of GDP at 32% and the government's investment contribution at 3%, private and local government investment would be 29%. Therefore, with an investment ratio of 32%, the portion of consumption as part of GDP is 68%. Of this figure, the government's budgeted portion for consumption would be over 13%, while private consumption would be 55%.

Simply put, if the capital–output ratio holds at the comparatively high current level of 4, then to realize average annual growth of 7% over the next 36 years with the trade surplus having fallen to zero, we must shift to domestic demand as the main driver of economic growth, we can still lower the investment rate from the almost

---

[4]Government investment here does not include a variety of extra-budgetary investments. The source of most of China's regional government investment is from extra-budgetary funds, such as income from land transfer payments and through debt capital via banks and the financial markets. For example, in 2010, local governments earned RMB2.8 trillion from land transfer payments. Of which, apart from the demolition and relocation costs of RMB1.67 trillion, most went towards agricultural and rural construction, urban construction and affordable housing projects totalling RMB1.02 trillion. In the same year, national and local government debt amounted to RMB10.72 trillion. Excluding the as yet unspent portion (10.3%) and the land purchase and reserve expenditure, investment in public welfare and infrastructure amounted to RMB9.27 trillion, accounting for 86.54% of total debt.

40% currently to 32%, and therefore, lifting the consumption rate from around 50% now to 68%. This type of investment and consumption structure will be consistent with more balanced development strategy with the focus of the people's livelihood. Table 5.2 illustrates this situation.

2. In Search of Endogenous Supernormal Purchasing Power

What scale of supernormal purchasing power does China require to see continued supernormal growth in the next 36 years? Based on the assumption that supernormal buying power accounts for 2% of GDP, if GDP in 2013 is about RMB50 trillion, then supernormal purchasing power should be RMB1 trillion; if GDP in 2049 is RMB570 trillion, then supernormal buying power should be RMB11.4 trillion. If we calculate the total accumulated purchasing power over 36 years, it would reach RMB170 trillion. That is, the average annual conventional economic growth rate over the next 36 years without taking into account supernormal purchasing power could reach 5%. This would rely mainly on upgrading consumption and industry, urbanization, informationalization and modernization of agriculture, which are promoted by conventional market forces. Adding supernormal purchasing power could increase average annual growth by 2 percentage points to 7%. To achieve this, supernormal purchasing power constituting a total investment capacity of RMB170 trillion will be required.

But where exactly will this massive supernormal buying power come from? On the one hand, solving the supply bottleneck and ecological construction will require raising a huge amount of funds; on the other hand, filling the vacuum left by international extraordinary buying power will also need the continued spending of massive amounts of funds. Evidently, the solution now lies in answering these two seemingly contradictory issues.

To solve the key issues of the bottlenecks in supply and the accumulation of ecological assets requires a long-term investment, with the returns uncertain and enterprises generally not willing to invest.

Table 5.2 The Composition of China's GDP with Supernormal Growth to 2049

Year	2013	2014	2015	2016	2017	2018	2023	2028	2033	2038	2043	2048	2049
Total investment (RMB trillion)	16.0	17.3	18.7	20.2	21.8	23.5	34.5	50.8	53.9	72.1	96.5	129.1	136.9
Percentage of GDP(%)	32	32	32	32	32	32	32	32	24	24	24	24	24
– Non-government investment	14.5	15.7	16.9	18.3	19.7	21.3	31.3	46.0	47.1	63.1	84.4	113.0	119.8
– Percentage of GDP (%)	29	29	29	29	29	29	29	29	21	21	21	21	21
– Government investment (RMB trillion)	1.5	1.6	1.8	1.9	2.0	2.2	3.2	4.8	6.7	9.0	12.1	16.1	17.1
– Percentage of GDP (%)	3	3	3	3	3	3	3	3	3	3	3	3	3
Total consumption (RMB trillion)	33.0	35.9	39.1	42.5	46.3	50.0	73.4	107.9	170.6	228.3	305.6	408.9	433.4
Percentage of GDP (%)	66	66.5	67	67.5	68	68	68	68	76	76	76	76	76
– Private consumption (RMB trillion)	26.5	28.9	31.5	34.3	37.4	40.4	59.3	87.3	141.4	189.3	253.3	338.9	359.3
– Percentage of GDP (%)	53	54	54	55	55	55	55	55	63	63	63	63	63
– Government consumption (RMB trillion)	6.5	7.0	7.6	8.2	8.8	9.5	14.0	20.6	29.2	39.1	52.3	69.9	74.1
– Percentage of GDP (%)	13	13	13	13	13	13	13	13	13	13	13	13	13

(*Continued*)

Table 5.2 (*Continued*)

Year	**2013**	**2014**	**2015**	**2016**	**2017**	**2018**	**2023**	**2028**	**2033**	**2038**	**2043**	**2048**	**2049**
Trade surplus (RMB trillion)	1.0	0.81	0.58	0.32	0.0	0.0	0.0	0.0	0.0	0.0	0.0	0.0	0.0
Percentage of GDP (%)	2	1.5	1	0.5	0	0	0	0	0	0	0	0	0
Total GDP (RMB trillion)	50.00	54.00	58.34	63.02	68.02	73.46	107.90	158.65	224.52	300.42	402.05	537.99	570.30

Note: GDP for 2013 refers to the end of 2012. The actual GDP value for that year was RMB51.93 trillion; the purpose of this table is to model the future and at the time it was created the annual data for 2012 had not yet been released. Therefore, for the sake of simplicity, GDP for 2013 is assumed at RMB50 trillion. Additionally, the shares of investment and spending as a percentage of GDP are also based on the analysis in the text and are assumed as follows: the investment ratio is set to fall from 32 to 24% by 2033; the consumption ratio will rise from 66 to 68% by 2017 and 76% by 2033; and the ratio of the trade surplus will fall from an initial 2% to zero by 2017 with imports and exports in balance.

But in fact, the defining characteristic of supernormal purchasing power is precisely long-term expenditure, without too much care for short term. This is because any kind of buying power that only seeks a return on investment will become conventional buying power and will have absolutely no supernormal effect on overall demand. Thus, only supernormal buying power can provide a source of funds needed for ecological construction and key strategic bottlenecks, and thereby concurrently solve the two difficult questions raised above.

But a major difficulty is finding a workable mechanism. Who will provide supernormal buying power? In what manner should it be provided so as to reap the effectiveness of supernormal buying power? If the market mechanism is unable to produce supernormal purchasing power, would government spending work instead? Clearly, it would not, as over-expenditure by the state would inevitably cause an extra-budgetary fiscal deficit. This, in turn, would bring about inflation thereby influencing conventional market operations, squeezing out conventional market investments and ultimately counteracting the positive effects of fiscal buying power. Therefore, it is impossible for conventional fiscal spending to provide real supernormal buying power.

Then, can China be like the Fed and provide supernormal buying power through excessive money supply? This is even more impossible. The renminbi is not an international currency like the dollar. Excessive issuance will inevitably lead to domestic inflation and undermine the stability of economic growth and the people's livelihood. More importantly, even if in the future, the renminbi was to make some progress toward internationalization, supernormal buying power still could not be created through excessive currency issuance. As stated in Chapter 3, the virtualization of the US economy in recent decades upon the basis of the dollar's supremacy, while producing short-term gains, the long-term after effects have been too big. In the decades in which the Fed provided supernormal buying power, although it did not bring about inflation and the dollar retained its place as the international currency, the long-term cost was the damage to the US real economy, the bubble in the financial industry and the country becoming debt-ridden. Ultimately, not only was this unsustainable, it created a deep crisis for long-term national development that is difficult to clean up.

So, where is China's endogenous effective supernormal buying power? Effective supernormal buying power should occur at the same time current levels of effective demand are increased, having no effect — or a "neutral" effect — on the normal operation of the market mechanism. In the process of implementation, expenditure from supernormal buying power should not have a major effect on the fiscal deficit and instead will take the form of normal income and profits of enterprises. At the end of the process, the results of supernormal buying power over the years will not only have avoided negatively affecting the long-term health of the national economy, but on the contrary, will have played a positive, constructive role. During annual operation of this effective supernormal buying power, the short- and medium-term investment returns could be disregarded, but in the long-term, this super buying power could take the form of effective assets and profitability, which can eventually return to normal and be integrated into the market system.

In view of this, a comprehensive national strategic investment fund (abbreviated to National Strategic Development Fund) must be established to carry out long-term investments in ecological assets and strategic resources while injecting supernormal buying power into conventional market operations; its establishment and operates the strategic asset base for national development.

For the National Strategic Development Fund to be successful in achieving the function of supernormal buying power, the following principle must be followed: (1) fund raising must not form a fiscal deficit; (2) investing the must not crowd out the opportunity for market-oriented investments; (3) the results of investment/allocation must be real assets necessary for long-term national development. The last two points are actually two sides of the same thing, with the key being to clearly define the areas of investment for the development fund.

3. Investment Areas for Supernormal Purchasing Power

The accumulation of ecological assets and key supply bottlenecks seen in the new stage of growth are the real base conditions for long-term national development and are the investment areas for the National Strategic Development Fund. Much of the following introduction of the ecological environment is based on the results of long years of research by Professor Deng Yingtao. Because of the complexity of the technology and industry, coupled with the varying opinions among experts, all of the numbers used are approximate calculations and are only intended to provide rough indications and scope. The goal is to illustrate the solvability of a number of major topics that must be addressed for China to achieve healthy, long-term development.[5]

(1) *Comprehensively Utilizing the Solar, Thermal, Land and Water Resources of the Tarim Basin*

Southern Xinjiang is a vast area with abundant natural resources including solar, thermal, land, minerals and oil, but most of the region is covered by desert, with annual rainfall only measuring in the tens of millimeters. It is difficult to develop the local economy, society and culture. The Taklamakan Desert covers a total area of 340,000 square kilometers (510 million mu), accounting for 47.3% of China's total desert area.

Sunshine is abundant in the Taklamakan Desert, with average annual sunshine of about more than 3,000 hours. But because of technical and cost constraints, it is unable to be fully utilized over

[5] Professor Deng Yingtao and partners Wang Xiaoqiang and Cui Hemin among others have spent years on an exhaustive search travelling over half of China in forming a theory and policy recommendation about a new method of development called "Rebuilding China." See Deng Yingtao, "Xin Fazhan Fangshi yu Zhongguo de Weilai [A New Development Model and China's Future]," Shanghai People's Press, 2013; "Xin Nengyuan Geming yu Fazhan Fangshi Yueqian," Shanghai People's Press, 2013; "Zai Zao Zhongguo, Zouxiang Weilai [Rebuilding China Into the Future]," Shanghai People's Press, 2013.

the long-term. Ground water resources are also extremely abundant, reaching 8 trillion cubic meters,[6] but most is brackish water, which traditionally is also unable to be utilized. Along with recent advances in technology, the advent of hollow ceramic flat solar panels has fundamentally solved the difficult problems of the high cost of manufacturing traditional solar panels and their short lifespan.[7] Through the construction of ceramic solar cells to generate electricity, the cost of every kilowatt hour (KWh) of power can be reduced to RMB0.15–RMB0.2, allowing for the large-scale desalination of brackish water and thereby stimulating the development of agriculture, industry, commerce and cities. It would offer hope of developing the more than 100 million mu of land into a habitable area upon which millions of people could live with massive amounts electricity output.

Professor Deng Yingtao among others concluded the following after exhaustive research:

> *In the area of land to the east of the Hotan River and west of the Taitema Lake, 50,000 square kilometers of ceramic panels could be laid out with gross power output of about 5 trillion watts (each square kilometer of ceramic panels produce about 100 million watts of power).*[8] *A portion of this power could be used to extract and desalinate the brackish water under the desert; another part of this energy could be used for pumped storage hydroelectricity, solving the problems of intermittent supply and volatility of*

---

[6] Expedition Team of the Taklamakan Desert, Chinese Academy of Sciences, "Takelamaganshamodiqu Shuiziyuan Pingjia yu Liyong [Water Resources Evaluation and Utilization in the Taklamakan Desert Areas]," Science Press, 1993.

[7] Cao Shuliang, "Dachicun hei ci fuhe taoci taiyangneng (shang, zhong, xia)," Diaocha Yanjiu Tongxun, 2009, No. 9–11.

[8] Every square meter of sunlight has a maximum radiant power of about 1 kilowatt, with the Taklamakan Desert able to get 0.8 kilowatts, while ceramic solar panels have an efficiency ratio of 5%, meaning that every square meter generates about 40 watts. With 3,000 hours of annual sunlight, every square meter can generate about 120 watts per year, and for the sake of a stable calculation, let us put that number at 100 watts, meaning that every square kilometer can generate 100 million watts of power per year.

solar power; the additional power can be used by local industry and agriculture and also for transmission elsewhere.[9]

The core of the process is illustrated in Figure 5.2.

According to Professor Deng Yingtao's theory, not only is this scheme workable from a technical point of view, its prospects also look very good from an economic perspective. In regards to investment, assuming the cost of every square meter of ceramic panel is about RMB100 (with a lifespan of 70 years), meaning that every square kilometer of paneling would cost RMB100 million, laying out 50,000 square meters would require an investment of RMB5 trillion. And while other aspects of the project such as pumping and desalination equipment, reservoirs and well as power transmission and water pipelines would also require large amounts of investment, they would still be insignificant compared to the costs of the ceramic panels. Simply put, we can assume the total fixed-asset investment would be within RMB6 trillion.

For the return on investment, first, the core annual output would include net production of 4 trillion watts of power, 30 billion cubic meters of desalinated water and 30 billion cubic meters of brackish water.[10] Assuming that every watt is priced at RMB0.4 and every square meter of fresh water at RMB2, even if we ignore the brackish water, then direct income from the core business would be more than RMB1.6 trillion. Second, relying on the core output of the above-mentioned power generation and desalination, the roughly 400 million mu of desert area in the Tarim Basin could be developed into fertile farmland, pastures and woodlands.

[9] Deng Yingtao, "Xin Nengyuan Geming yu Fazhan Fangshi Yueqian," Shanghai People's Press, 2013, p. 154.

[10] 50,000 square kilometers of ceramic panels produce 5 trillion watts of power annually. Of that amount, 36 billion watts would be used for pumping up the brackish groundwater, 90 billion watts would be used for desalination and power storage needs would account for 640 billion watts for an estimated net annual output of around 4.2 trillion watts.

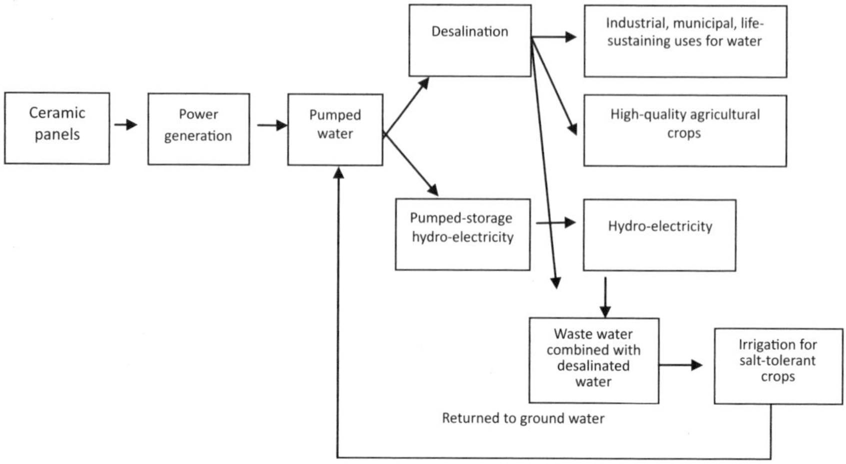

Figure 5.2 The Core Process of Transforming Desert Lands.

Not only could they be used to produce cotton, high-quality melons and fruits, timber, livestock and other agricultural, forestry and animal products, it could also spur on the development of agriculture processing industries, such as the producers of cotton textiles, food, leather, wool, animal feed and lumber. Additionally, the brackish water can be used to directly irrigate the other more than 100 million mu of land to grow Jerusalem artichokes, salicornia and other salt-tolerant plants that could in turn produce 20 million to 30 million metric tons of high-energy fuel (2,5-dimethylfuran), and in turn further develop the region's bio-based chemical industry.[11]

Again, the development of agriculture and animal husbandry and industry will necessarily lead to people to populate the area and the development of towns. Professor Deng Yingtao predicts that southern Xinjiang could add 10 million people, bringing the total population to 20 million, with around 90% of people living in towns and the other 10% accounted for by the agriculture sector working

[11] See Deng Yingtao, "Xinnengyuan Geming yu Fazhan Fangshi Yueqian," Shanghai People's Press, 2013, pp. 157–160.

a land area of 400 million mu and achieving a modern economy of scale. New immigration is the root of the development plan for southern Xinjiang. Not only can it change the composition of the local population, it can at the same time raise the level of salaries and improve the people's lives. As the population increases and more enterprises establish themselves, southern Xinjiang will gradually begin to prosper. In the end, through the irrigation provided for agriculture, forestry, animal husbandry and crops and transpiration from the crops, it may be possible to improve the average level of humidity on the Tarim Basin, causing the majority of the desert area to gradually become an oasis, effectively altering the desert climate. If this can be achieved, it will be for the enduring benefit of future generations.

(2) *Shuotian Canal — The Western Water Diversion Plan*

The source of China's water resources is in the west and looking at the topographic layout, areas in the west are elevated and low in the east while land in the south is high and flat in the north. Originally, the pattern of higher elevations in the west and lower levels in the east benefitted the west-to-east diversion of water, but the interlocking barrier of the Himalayas, Hengduan and Bayan Har mountains force the waters first south and then east again before finally ending up in the Yellow River flowing through the northwest. Thus, starting from the west on a south–north water diversion project is the basis to solving China's water resource problem. After Professor Guo Kai proposed water diversion from the Yarlung Tsangpo River in the "Shuotian Project," many experts proposes a number of different accompanying support plans. However, because the construction of dams and canals face many geological, energy and other technical difficulties, the plans were grounded. Now, two major technologies have made breakthroughs in China: first, the vertical axis wind turbine technology has enabled significant reduction in the cost of power generation; second, super-long tunnelling and large-scale bridge and culvert technologies (domestically-made tunnel boring machines have diameters of up to 13 meters) are already widely used, meaning that aqueducts need not take the high, winding routes along the contours between two mountains and can instead pass directly through them. Therefore, wind turbine power plants of varying scale could be constructed in locations dispersed across the north–south ranges of the Hengduan Mountains, which boast the many topographical advantages of the valley winds. They would not require power transformers, transmission or grid management and gradually use the power generated by the wind to pump the water. After traversing a watershed, it can all flow naturally to the surface through artesian aquifers. Thus, by combining the technologies of wind power to pump the water and tunnelling and culvert building to transport the water, the western water diversion project would be feasible.

Professor Deng Yingtao concluded:

> *Guo Kai's "Shuotian Canal" concept would be for 70% to 80% of its total length be an open channel diverting 200 billion cubic meters of water, or the equivalent of three to four Yellow Rivers. And with the complexities and ever changing geological nature of the Hengduan Mountain ranges and winding thousands of kilometers, it is very hard to imagine with the technology available today. Open channels that are overly long are dangerous and the geology is unstable with fault belts occurring between mountains, making construction difficult. Also, each stage must connect up to the next to flow into one river, crisscrossing each other making the maintenance too risky. If there was a super-cheap wind-powered water pump, added to which were super-long tunnels and large-scale culverts, the entire water diversion project could be split up and spread out: where the wind is strong, wind turbine power plants could be built; where the terrain and geology is good, build a reservoir, pump the water and store it. There's no need to build a sensationally, awe inspiring large dam that could store tens of billions of cubic meters of water. To divert water to the north, it doesn't have to be concentrated into one pipeline. The main open channel can be greatly shortened and the amount of water can be significantly lessened and can be separated out into many small and medium-sized reservoirs and canals, one section at a time. Where the terrain and geology is advantageous, large dams and canals can be built. Where they are not good, smaller dams and canals are suitable. Some may be directly connected, others not. When it*

comes to crossing over rivers, it can be separated out over many pumping stations, many routes and directions.[12]

In conclusion, from a technical perspective, there are not any major problems with the western water diversion project, it is just that the costs of the investment are massive. However, once constructed the benefits to society, the economy and ecology will be huge and impossible to estimate.

First, it will solve the issues of water conservancy in the Yellow River. The western water diversion will supply 200 billion cubic meters of water annually (the Yellow River's annual discharge is around 50 billion cubic meters), guaranteeing the Yellow River's perennial discharge of 2,500 square meters per second and allowing vessels of 100,000 tons to ply the waterway between Zhengzhou and the mouth of the river.

Second, there will be remarkable potential for land reclamation. Once the Yellow River becomes a subterranean watercourse, it will save almost 20 million mu of flood plains and estuarine mud flats, which can be made suitable for other uses. At the same time, because superabsorbent resin technology is very mature, it is technically feasible to transform sandy wastelands. As soon as northern and north–western areas of China have water, almost 2 billion mu of wasteland will no longer have to lie idle and the ecological conditions will gradually improve.

Third, wind-generated electricity will be massive. According to estimates, the Shuotian Canal's combined hydro and thermal electric power generation will have an installed capacity of 276 million kilowatts, or roughly equivalent to 10-times the output of the Three Gorges power project, while the cost of construction would be cheaper.

Fourth, it would attract a large amount of labor. For this epic engineering project to get started would require over 10 million workers and related support and logistics staff added to which

---

[12] Deng Yingtao and Wang Xiaoqiang, "Weile Duoshu Rende Xiandaihua," Oriental Morning Post, April 10, 2012.

would be the labor needed to work the more than 1 billion mu of wasteland. The Shuotian Canal itself would need communication, education, cultural and medical staff as well offering employment positions within the power generation industry and the newly established tourist areas. Along the banks of the canal that will span many thousands of kilometers will be ports and towns that will attract populations. The employment opportunities that the entire western water diversion project will create are unparalleled. In fact, in the US, the Tennessee Valley Authority project started long ago and was the first example of a massive national-level project to improve the ecology, create jobs and increase the value of assets.

(3) *The Structure Change of Energy Economics*

As mentioned earlier, China's current energy economic model that is comprised mainly of coal, crude oil and other mineral fuels is unsustainable. By 2050, with the full realization of modernization, average annual per capita energy use and total overall energy demand will increase by five or six times. If we rely purely on international oil, international politics will surely cause some major troubles; if we rely mainly on coal then there will certainly be an ecological disaster. Thus, we can only resolutely change the traditional energy structure's overreliance on coal, crude oil and other fossil fuels to one in which we maximize the use of renewables as part of a more balanced and diversified energy mix. The following passage will mainly discuss the development and utilization of renewable energy including hydropower, wind power, biomass energy and solar energy, all of which have massive potential.

According to analysis by Professor Deng Yingtao,[13] the potential of China's renewable energy can be summarized as follows:

Hydropower — installed capacity of 400 million kilowatts, annual usage 4,000 hours, power generation 1.6 trillion watts; no technical issues.

---

[13] See Deng Yingtao, "Xinnengyuan Geming yu Fazhan Fangshi Yueqian," Shanghai People's Press, 2013.

Wind power — about 1 billion kilowatts can be developed on land and in shallow coastal waters with installed capacity of 400 million kilowatts, annual usage of 3,000 hours, generating about 1.2 trillion watts; the technology is basically mature.

Biomass energy — straw from crops, waste from woodlands as well as grass that can be planted across 100 million hectares of marginal land can produce about 2.67 billion tons of standard biomass briquettes. Additionally, by 2050 about 5 billion tons of animal manure (500 million tons calculated on a dry basis), can produce biogas that can generate 225 billion watts. Technical issues include modernizing the compression moulding technology, using high-efficient coal burning and Denmark straw-burning technologies for power generation to replace coal-burning generation. These are either already in use or are basically mature technologies.

Not including solar power, the total renewable energy mentioned above converts to about 3.7 billion tons of standard coal equivalent. According to the above calculation, by 2050 China's total energy demand will be about 7.5 billion tons of coal equivalent, so if the above renewable energy development takes place, it would account for about 50% of total demand. Also, as the above technologies are basically mature, or at least there are no fundamental obstacles, the main requirement are the massive funds for long-term investment, with advances in technology and increasing scale lowering costs.

Solar power — China's total solar radiation is around 1.2 trillion kilowatts. In the field of concentrated solar power, internationally the two technologies for photovoltaic and concentrated photovoltaic power stations are not yet completely mature, but advances happen very quickly, with a fundamental breakthrough not far away. There is a relatively large gap when comparing China with advanced international levels, which is especially clear in regards to engineering scalability and commercialization. But in terms of resources, there is at least 40,000 square kilometers of land in the Tengger and Badain Jaran deserts between Inner Mongolia, Gansu, and Ningxia that is suitable for the construction of large-area photovoltaic power plants (this area could also be used to provide complimentary wind power). In eastern Xinjiang's Turpan–Hami Basin and Lop Nor areas, there is at least 40,000 square kilometers upon which concentrated solar power (thermal) stations could be constructed. These two projects combined could have a total combined installed capacity reaching about 3 billion kilowatts, with annual generating output of more than 4 trillion watts. Added to the 5 trillion watts generated by the photovoltaic panels in the Tarim Basin, solar power could generate more than 9 trillion watts.

Apart from the large-scale concentrated solar power plants, utilization of distributive solar power technology is becoming increasingly mature, including solar hot water heaters and residential solar power, whose development potential is massive.[14] If we add biogas from the biomass energy mix, then dispersal of renewable energy could play a major role in solving the problem of supplying power to the hundreds of millions in county-level areas and other smaller regions.[15]

Clearly, investment in utilization of solar energy will be huge and unprecedented. First is the investment required for the technical research. Next comes all the aspects of the actual construction of the power plant, power storage, the grid and transmission, which would need an investment of RMB1 trillion. But the multifaceted benefits of this project would be unparalleled. For a start, if many different means are used to achieve economical use of solar energy, China's power problem could be fundamentally solved. Second, solar electric

---

[14] Residential solar power, or Green Buildings, is an important fulcrum of the new energy revolution. In US futurist Jeremy Rifkin's "The Third Industrial Revolution; How Lateral Power is Transforming Energy, the Economy, and the World" (Palgrave Macmillan, 2011). Chinese edition: "Disanci Gongye Geming — Xinjingji Moshi Ruhe Gaibian Shijie" (CITIC Press Group, 2012) he takes the concept that "every building is a mini-power plant" as "the third industrial revolution" (actually it is the new energy revolution) as a major pillar.

[15] Professor Deng Yingtao cites a prediction by Professor Weng Shilie that the roof area of China's residential buildings cover an area in excess of 10 billion square meters. If rooftop solar power installations became widespread and optimized, they could produce a limitless supply of heat and energy. See Deng Yingtao, "Xinnengyuan Geming yu Fazhan Fangshi Yueqian," Shanghai People's Press, 2013, p. 74.

power rarely causes pollutant emissions, so its reduction of greenhouse gases and dust emissions caused by thermal power would be in the billions of tons. It would be astronomical. It would have fundamental significance to the improvement of the quality of China's environment.

Altogether, the prospects for utilizing renewable energy are vast. If we calculate that solar power generates about 4 trillion watts, we can convert that into 1.3 billion tons of standard coal equivalent. Adding about 3.7 billion tons of standard coal equivalent from hydropower, wind power and biomass energy, total renewable energy including solar power could amount to about 5 billion tons of standard coal equivalent, accounting for more than 66% of total national energy demand in 2050. Accordingly, when coal, crude oil, nuclear power and other forms of mineral energy is only one-third of China's overall energy mix, they would convert to more than 2 billion tons of standard coal equivalent, even less than China's 2011 coal production. This implies that although China must greatly increase the per capita energy usage level to achieve overall modernization, as long as the necessary long-term investment and research and development support is guaranteed, then China's inexhaustible renewable energy can be rationally developed. Then, China will achieve self-reliance and sustainability for its energy supply while avoiding creating a burden on global energy politics and also controlling China's environmental costs at below current levels and thus making a decisive contribution to the construction of a global ecological civilization.

(4) *Human Resources Development and the New Demographic Dividend*

Human capital is the number one factor in modernizing technology and developing enterprises. The importance of this is self-evident. Amongst all kinds of human capital, top-level talent development in fundamental research and cutting-edge science has already received widespread attention in China. The government has even especially developed a long-term national-level innovation platform and related policies. By contrast, practical human capital has not yet received sufficient attention.

The development of practical human capital mainly refers to the training of professional, skilled workers. This mission involves, transforming the legions of manual laborers, who currently number in the hundreds of millions, into skilled proficient workers and professional white collar and service industry employees industry employees, is necessary and important to china's industrial upgrading. According to research, while the US is the global leader in terms of state-of-the-art technology, its basic industrial technology is not at the same level as that in Germany or Japan. A very important reason German and Japanese manufacturing industries are unmatched globally is a strong and advanced vocational training system for skilled workers.[16]

In Germany, through participation and support of the government and enterprise in the vocational education system, a complete training structure for ordinary workers was formed. Through an effective screening and grooming system, vocational skills training can be provided to young people, offering them jobs related to their proficiencies. Through training, ordinary workers could master the required skills and thus become qualified and quality participants in the high-end manufacturing industry. This would not only ensure the competitiveness of the manufacturing industry, it would also effectively lift the incomes of the entire working class.

As China is a populous developing nation, a strong manufacturing industry is the key to modernization, while enhancing the business format and level of the service sector stems from the demands of upgraded consumption. Therefore, building a professional, skilled workforce is a strategic issue for long-term national competitiveness and must be comprehensively planned and speedily promoted.

---

[16] J. Hage and M. Garnier, "Education and Economic Growth in Germany," in Corwin (ed.), Research in Education and Stratification, Volume 9, Greenwich, Conn.: J.A.I. Press, 1990; J. Hage, B. Fuller and M. Garnier, "The Active State and the Coupling of Education and Economic Growth: France," *American Sociological Review*, December, 1988.

Germany's Basic Law of education" clearly states that the costs of vocational education should be 1.1% of GDP.[17] Germany's 2011 nominal GDP was 2.59 trillion euros, and its vocational training fees were about 28.5 billion euros, which could be used to educate 2 million people, or about 2.5% of the total population. Currently, vocational schools in Germany allocate about 15,000 euros annually per student for training.[18]

Referencing Germany's experience, assuming China had a two-year and three-year formal vocational training system, and students made up 2% of the population, or about 26 million people, every year there would be about 10 million newly enrolled students and 10 million graduates. Assuming that the average lost per student for the training was RMB15,000, the annual vocational training cost would be about RMB390 billion. In 20 years, China would have added 200 million highly-skilled workers, technicians and professional, high-quality service-oriented employees that have received systematic training, fundamentally ensuring the realization of industrial upgrading and consumption upgrading.

As we can see from the international experience, to carry out a more reasonable income distribution under a market economy, a large-scale improvement in the skills and level of professionalism of the basic labor force must be done, which will thus increase the level of their income.[19] In this way, a large number of the workforce can be upgraded from simple manual laborers to skilled, professional, modernized human resources and fundamentally improve the income distribution situation in China, narrowing the income gap.

But where will this large-scale injection of fund come from? The finance for Germany's vocational training system are guaranteed

---

[17] Zhang Hongzhi, "Zhengfu Shuxing Zhiyejiaoyu Zhizhe de Guoji Zuowei Fanshi Ji Qishi," *Jiaoyu Xueshu Yuekan* [Education Research Monthly] 2011, Number 10.

[18] Duan Yuqing, "Deguo Zhiyejiaoyu Jingfei Baozhangtixi Dui Woguo Xibu Zhiyejiaoyu de Qishi," *Jiaoyu Caihui Yuanjiu*, 2012, No. 2.

[19] This phenomena can be explained from the perspective of Marxism's political economy theory. See Meng Jie, "Laodong yu Ziben zai Jiazhichuanzaozhong de Zhengheguanxi Yanjiu [The Positive-sum Relations Between Capital and Labor in the Creation of Value]," *Economic Research Journal*, 2011. No. 4.

through a diverse model, with both public and private financing, including direct subsidies from enterprises, non-enterprise fund raising, mixed fee subsidies, state subsidies and personal subsidies.[20] China can further improve with a vocational education fund under the National Strategic Development Fund, and with local governments and enterprises jointly providing funds for vocational education in line with the principle of human resource capitalization. With the reasonable allocation of profits generated from increased manufacturing efficiency, it would make the expenditure on education be transformed into an investment.

Currently, apart from local governments opening vocational training academies, private enterprises have also been setting up for-profit training institutions one after the other. The involvement of the National Strategic Development Fund should focus on improving and increasing the pace of expansion of the overall system already in place. In terms of funding, the National Strategic Development Fund, local governments, private enterprises and non-profit training organizations could work together in a variety of complimentary aspects, step-by-step providing training for all of the nation's workers. This would become a joint investment between the National Strategic Development Fund and local governments in the fundamental asset of vocational education.

In summary, from the comprehensive development of resources in southern Xinjiang and the western water diversion project to the restructuring of the energy mix, utilization of renewable energy and the accumulation of human capital, all look feasible and promising for the National Strategic Development Fund. In other fields, from land improvement to development of the South China Sea, from the applied research and development system used in upgrading industry to the marine economy and national defence construction, these are even more super projects that are worthy of national-level strategic investment. Due to space limitations, I am unable to go into great detail on each of them, so the above projects serve only as examples.

---

[20] Gao Li, "Deguo Zhiyejiaoyu yu Peixunjingfei de Laiyuan," *Shijie Zhiye Jishujiaoyu*, 2005, No. 1.

4. Creating the National Strategic Development Fund

To make a state strategic investment valued in the hundreds of trillions of *renminbi* become supernormal buying power, real and effective demand must be created that does not cause additional pressure on the fiscal deficit. The key is in the establishment and operation of the fund. In principle, the National Strategic Development Fund should be positioned as a quasi-market fund with standardized operations, which will be backed by state credit and shoulder the responsibility of national strategic tasks. The main points are as follows: a number of specialized sub-funds should be established under the National Strategic Development Fund; the central government can provide the guidance funds through state financing and authorize the fund special scope for financing and investment, selectively provide state credit guarantees, and make market-oriented selection of fund managers; use a multitude of tools and channels to raise funds domestically and abroad, creating a market-oriented, professional fund operation team; make a compounded, long-term incentive mechanism that includes both national glory and long-term economic benefits; build a well-constructed operating system for investment decision-making, consultation and audit, which will lead to the effective overall operation of the fund.

(1) *Umbrella Fund Structure*

It would be impossible for a long-term, strategic fund in the RMB100 trillion category to be just a single entity. It could only be incorporated in a system of many sub-funds. First, different sub-funds can be established for investments in different areas. For example, for desert management, a southern Xinjiang comprehensive development fund could be established; for the western water diversion, a "Shuotian Project" fund; a national vocational education fund for labor force training; and for affordable housing, a national housing development fund. Second, a number of similar funds could be established in the same investment areas and depending on the situation, appropriately divide up the labor with a moderate amount of competition to facilitate mutual learning and comparative assessment.

(2) *Introduction of Capital and Public Fund Raising*

Funds in the 100 trillion renminbi category cannot rely solely on state finances. But even with decades of investment cycles, it would still be difficult to attract public investors in the same way as ordinary market products, and therefore requires careful capital structure design and risk allocation. The following points could be considered when setting it up: (1) Fiscal guidance funds. As the initial capital reflects the fund as part of national strategy, in principle contributions from state finances would be about 10% of the fund's scale. These funds would not come from conventional national fiscal expenditures, but from the accumulated massive public capital investments among the large-sized state owned enterprises;[21] (2) Cornerstone investor contributions. This type of the investors come from those with credibility and strength and share the same outlook for China's long-term development prospects. Their affiliation does not just include the contribution of funds, it also increases the public confidence in the fund and its appeal. Raising funds from this type of investor requires the soft support of the nation to achieve more than 15% of the fund's scale; (3) Contributions from ordinary public investors. We can use the current management of private equity as a reference, only raising funds from accredited qualified investors. These contributions could account for more than 15% of the fund. The categories above must bear the investment risk. (4) Fund companies issue corporate bonds to small-and-medium sized investors and special bonds in the interbank market. These two types do not necessarily need to

[21] In regards to how the assets of large state-owned enterprises can be transferred for use as sustained investment to benefit the nation's people and create social capital, this author has published, "Kanbujian de suoyouzhe: xiandai qiye de quan gemeng" "the invisible owner: the ownership revolution in modern industrial enterprises".

assume risk with the investment principal and income agreement guaranteed firstly from the priority arrangements in fund income distribution and supplemented by combinations of commercial insurance and the state guaranteeing the bottom line. These types of debt securities could account for 50%. In this way, a multi-layered funding structure can be created, as is shown in Figure 5.3. Different types of funding assumes different degrees of risk, which is more in line with the reality of the market operation.

(3) *Fund Management Team and the Incentive Structure*

The long-term operation of a strategic fund necessarily requires a special management team. This includes, first, talented individuals with knowledge of national affairs and in-depth management experience in government and industry. For example, people from high-level positions in government ministries, commissions, offices and bureaus or corporations, including retirees who are still suitable; second, professional talents who have worked in equity investment, management consulting and capital markets among others. These individuals would mainly be sought from among

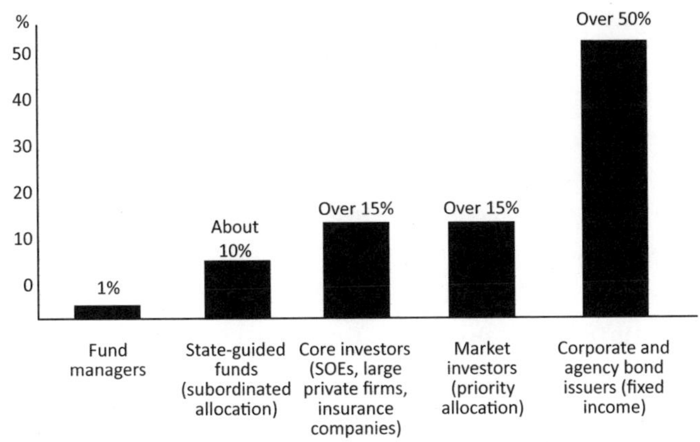

Figure 5.3 The Multilayered Structure of the National Strategic Development Fund.

Note: The percentages in the diagram serve as a rough illustration and are not accurate values and therefore do not add up to 100%.

domestic and international professional institutions and would be offered an appropriate, effective, long-term incentive system. In this regard, the investment banking and private equity industries both have banking and private equity industries both have quite standard routines and schemes. However.....disadvantages of excessive incentives and should be implemented only. However, there are disadvantages when the material incentives are excessive and they should be identified through thorough research and implemented only after being appropriately modified to ensure the management team's attractiveness to talented individuals and its operational vitality.

(4) *Fund Investment Decisions and Project Consultation System*

The investment orientation of the National Strategic Development Fund will have been preset, but contingent decisions on specific projects and investment cases will be handled by the fund's management team. Lessons can be drawn from the investment committee system in the investment industry. Because many projects involved will be long-term, cross-regional and large in scale, the complexity of the technological, environmental, energy and social aspects will be unprecedented and therefore require a high-quality integrated decision-making advisory system. The Issuance Examination Committee system of the China Securities Regulatory Commission can be studied. A national inventory can be collated to establish a database of qualified consultants and then an impartial method can be used to form different categories of consultative committees to serve as authorized consultants for the different funds for a specified period. At the same time, there must be an external audit of the fund's operations, using state auditors or some private third party.

(5) *Expectations of the Fund's Return on Investment*

The National Strategic Development Fund's internal system acts as supernormal purchasing power, appearing as investments. And as long as it is properly operated, they will become long-term investments with excellent returns. For example:

Land reclamation — reclamation of the Taklamakan Desert. Even if we only take into account a core area of 10,000 square kilometers, successful transformation will create a production base of 100 million mu for the cultivation of high-quality grains, cotton, fruit and vegetables as well dozens of medium-sized towns. Added to this would be the management of small watersheds, rivers and the transformation into farmland in areas across the country, all of which can be linked with land reclamation. Just as long as there is appropriate investment, the outlook for the addition of new land is very positive. This land replacement (for example the 100 million mu) can be used over the next 30 years for urbanization, with the areas where the towns replace agriculture increasing the value of the land. For example, if every mu is worth RMB1 million, then it will be worth up to RMB1 trillion.

Water diversion and conservancy — the results of the western water diversion project could reach over 100 billion cubic meters of water annually; the comprehensive spread of modern agricultural irrigation and water conservancy technology projects will also bring about massive water saving benefits. Based on a calculation of 100 billion cubic meters of water per year, if every cubic meter was priced cheaply at RMB2 per liter, that would mean every year it would generate income of RMB200 billion. Also the improvement to agriculture, industrial production and the people's livelihood in northern China from the north-south water diversion would bring about economic benefits that are even more impossible to measure.

Affordable social housing — when the population reaches 1.5 billion people, 500 million housing units will be required, of which 30%, or at least 150 million units, will be affordable social housing. Of that number, assuming 100 million units are invested by the fund, over 20 years of construction, the fund will hold them and then lease them out to qualified renters. As rental prices would be below the market level, initial rents would be low and profits small. But as urbanization and *gentrification* spreads, rents will inevitably increase steadily, added to which the fund can implement a unified plan for the commercial management of the residential compounds. If this is properly planned, looking at a 30-year period, the affordable social housing project not only can provide a basis of material security upon which a harmonious society can be built, but also ultimately turn it into a quality asset.

Skilled, professional work force — using the above-mentioned calculations of 10 million graduates every year for 20 years, creating a skilled, professional work force of 200 million people, it not only produces a new demographic dividend, but solely in terms of the increase in personal incomes and personal income taxes would also be astronomical.

We can see that the National Strategic Development Fund's ability to invest in the development of a strategic foundation is also feasible in regards to investment returns. As long as the fund's management operation reaches a mid-level (not a high level), with an RMB100-trillion level fund investing cumulatively over a span of 30 years, it will open up unprecedented long-term, stable investment opportunities. This not only will help China's economic growth continue to hold onto its leading position globally, but also fundamentally reshape the nation's landscape and be an unprecedented achievement.

Appendix

Table A.1 China Investment and Consumption:1978–2011

Year	Consumption				Investment		
	Final consumption rate(%)	Total consumption (billion RMB)	Consumption Growth rate(%)	Real consumption per capita (RMB)	Capital formation rate(%)	Total investment (billion RMB)	Investment growth rate(%)
1978	62.10	1356.573513		1409.295248	38.20	834.478393	
1979	64.40	1513.735067	11.56	1551.880284	36.10	848.537825	1.66
1980	65.50	1659.898031	9.68	1681.675732	34.80	881.900023	3.96
1981	67.10	1789.601361	7.81	1788.313775	32.50	866.796486	–1.71
1982	66.50	1934.231528	8.08	1902.75988	31.90	927.84941	7.04
1983	66.40	2140.928986	10.69	2078.410401	32.80	1057.56733	13.98
1984	65.80	2443.555164	14.14	2341.534506	34.20	1270.05451	20.09
1985	66.00	2781.036392	13.81	2627.312347	38.10	1605.41646	26.41
1986	64.90	2976.606391	7.03	2768.755886	37.50	1719.91895	7.13
1987	63.60	3254.864315	9.35	2977.917946	36.30	1857.72916	8.01
1988	63.90	3639.117063	11.81	3277.716088	37.00	2107.15699	13.43
1989	64.50	3822.540299	5.04	3391.663383	36.60	2169.06938	2.94
1990	62.50	3846.209859	0.62	3364.041755	34.90	2147.72359	–0.98
1991	62.40	4192.532226	9.00	3619.775197	34.80	2338.14297	8.87
1992	62.40	4789.578429	14.24	4087.682472	36.60	2809.27196	20.15

(Continued)

Table A.1 (*Continued*)

	Consumption				Investment		
Year	**Final consumption rate(%)**	**Total consumption (billion RMB)**	**Consumption Growth rate(%)**	**Real consumption per capita (RMB)**	**Capital formation rate(%)**	**Total investment (billion RMB)**	**Investment growth rate(%)**
1993	59.30	5187.239211	8.30	4376.789162	42.60	3726.41468	32.65
1994	58.20	5756.957002	10.98	4803.468504	40.50	4006.12987	7.51
1995	58.10	6374.93108	10.73	5263.274807	40.30	4421.85409	10.38
1996	59.20	7145.743185	12.09	5838.550184	38.80	4683.35871	5.91
1997	59.00	7783.699918	8.93	6296.167406	36.70	4841.7252	3.38
1998	59.60	8478.780986	8.93	6796.018777	36.20	5149.86362	6.36
1999	61.10	9354.502438	10.33	7436.839106	36.20	5542.27477	7.62
2000	62.30	10342.41859	10.56	8160.149748	35.30	5860.1505	5.74
2001	61.40	11039.06183	6.74	8649.472159	36.50	6562.30874	11.98
2002	59.60	11688.62477	5.88	9099.534284	37.80	7413.25531	12.97
2003	56.90	12277.84923	5.04	9500.993781	41.00	8846.95639	19.34
2004	54.40	12922.22306	5.25	9941.089225	43.00	10214.2572	15.46
2005	53.00	14013.56149	8.45	10717.33725	41.50	10972.8831	7.43
2006	50.80	15134.56164	8.00	11513.7253	41.70	12423.4492	13.22
2007	49.60	16869.83683	11.47	12767.70189	41.60	14148.8954	13.89
2008	48.60	18122.30274	7.42	13646.10679	43.80	16332.4457	15.43

2009	48.50	19751.40323	8.99	14800.60189	47.20	19221.9842	17.69
2010	48.20	21679.89309	9.76	16168.0449	48.10	21634.9141	12.55
2011	49.10	24137.37707	11.34	17914.70447	48.30	23744.1001	9.75
Average	59.56		9.15		38.51		10.92
Annual compounded growth rate for the period		9.12		7.76		10.68	

Note: Total consumption and total investment take 2012 as the base year for constant prices. Tatal consumption combines government consumption with househodl consumption. The final consumption rate is the proportion of real GDP it accouts for in that year.

Source: National Bureau of Statistics of China, "China Statistical Yearbook 2012," China Statistics Press, 2012.

Table A.2 China's Capital–Output Ratio: 1978–2010

Year	Real GDP (Billion RMB)	Real investment (Billion RMB)	Year	Real GDP (Billion RMB)	Real investment (Billion RMB)
1978	21844.984	8344.784	1995	109723.426	44218.541
1979	23505.203	8485.378	1996	120705.121	46833.587
1980	25341.955	8819.000	1997	131927.117	48417.252
1981	26670.661	8667.965	1998	142261.426	51498.636
1982	29086.188	9278.494	1999	153101.513	55422.748
1983	32242.906	10575.673	2000	166009.929	58601.505
1984	37136.097	12700.545	2001	179789.281	65623.087
1985	42136.915	16054.165	2002	196117.865	74132.553
1986	45864.505	17199.189	2003	215779.424	88469.564
1987	51177.112	18577.292	2004	237540.865	102142.572
1988	56950.189	21071.570	2005	264406.821	109728.831
1989	59264.191	21690.694	2006	297924.442	124234.492
1990	61539.358	21477.236	2007	340117.678	141488.954
1991	67188.016	23381.430	2008	372886.888	163324.457
1992	76756.065	28092.720	2009	407245.427	192219.842
1993	87474.523	37264.147	2010	449790.313	216349.141
1994	98916.787	40061.299	2011	491596.274	237441.001

Year	GDP growth (Billion RMB)	Investment growth (Billion RMB)	Capital–output
1978–1987	35105.205	118702.485	3.381
1988–1997	85311.237	332508.474	3.898
1998–2007	230625.462	871342.942	3.778
2001–2010	311806.994	1277713.492	4.098
1978–2010	469751.290	1894447.341	4.033

Note: In calculating the capital–output ratio, it is difficult to predict when an investment in any given year will yield results. It can be simplified by using the total investment for the 10-year period and the increase in the one-year lag total for 10-year GDP figure to calculate the average 10-year capital–output ratio. There are other methods for estimating capital–output ratio. Here, we will mainly focus on the overall performance of a single economic entity over a comparatively long period. Tables A.3 and A.4 will do the same.

Source: National Bureau of Statistics of China, "China Statistical Yearbook 2012," China Statistics Press, 2012. Real GDP and real investment data take 1990 as the base year for constant prices.

Table A.3 US Capital–Output Ratio:1965–2010

Year	Real GDP (US$1 billion)	Real investment (US$1 billion)	Year	Real GDP (US$1 billion)	Real investment (US$1 billion)
1965	3,607.00	435.7	1988	7,607.40	984.9
1966	3,842.10	474.1	1989	7,879.20	1,024.40
1967	3,939.20	452.4	1990	8,027.10	989.9
1968	4,129.90	478.7	1991	8,008.30	909.4
1969	4,258.20	506.6	1992	8,280.00	983.1
1970	4,266.30	473.4	1993	8,516.20	1,070.90
1971	4,409.50	527.3	1994	8,863.10	1,216.40
1972	4,643.80	589.8	1995	9,086.00	1,254.30
1973	4,912.80	658.9	1996	9,425.80	1,365.30
1974	4,885.70	610.3	1997	9,845.90	1,535.20
1975	4,875.40	502.2	1998	10,274.70	1,688.90
1976	5,136.90	603.7	1999	10,770.70	1,837.60
1977	5,373.10	694.9	2000	11,216.40	1,963.10
1978	5,672.80	778.7	2001	11,337.50	1,825.20
1979	5,850.10	803.5	2002	11,543.10	1,800.40
1980	5,834.00	715.2	2003	11,836.40	1,870.10
1981	5,982.10	779.6	2004	12,246.90	2,058.20
1982	5,865.90	670.3	2005	12,623.00	2,172.30
1983	6,130.90	732.8	2006	12,958.50	2,231.80
1984	6,571.50	948.7	2007	13,206.40	2,159.50
1985	6,843.40	939.8	2008	13,161.90	1,939.80
1986	7,080.50	933.5	2009	12,757.90	1,458.10
1987	7,307.00	962.2	2010	13,063.00	1,658.00
			2011	13,299.10	1,744.00

Year	GDP growth (US$1 billion)	Investment growth (US$1 billion)	Capital–output ratio
1965–1974	1,268.40	5207.2	4.105
1975–1984	1,968.00	7229.6	3.674
1985–1994	2,242.60	10014.5	4.466
1995–2004	3,977.00	17,198.30	4.324
2005–2009	440	9,961.50	22.64
1965–2010	9,692.10	51,269.10	5.29

Source: Bureau of Economic Analysis, "GDP and other major NIPA series, 1929–2012: II," August 2012. Real GDP and real investment use 2005 the base year for constant prices.

Table A.4 Japan's Capital–Output Ratio: 1980–2010

Year	Real GDP (1 billion yen)	Real investment (1 billion yen	Year	Real GDP (1 billion yen)	Real investment (1 billion yen
1980	2,69,833.88	86721.91	1996	4,67,345.70	133730.97
1981	2,81,104.42	87322.28	1997	4,74,802.70	133353.09
1982	2,90,596.21	86504.68	1998	4,65,291.70	121441.13
1983	2,99,490.60	83255.39	1999	4,64,364.30	114841.94
1984	3,12,859.56	86574.5	2000	4,74,847.20	119210.39
1985	3,32,674.07	93790.8	2001	4,76,535.10	115817.09
1986	3,42,092.33	95652.44	2002	4,77,914.80	107334.88
1987	3,56,143.52	101479.53	2003	4,85,968.30	108852.04
1988	3,81,596.01	116997.34	2004	4,97,440.80	111944.08
1989	4,02,088.29	127976.66	2005	5,03,921.00	113210.89
1990	4,24,494.26	138079.49	2006	5,12,452.00	116229.24
1991	4,38,605.89	141463.56	2007	5,23,685.80	119840.26
1992	4,42,198.20	135210.94	2008	5,18,230.90	119073.91
1993	4,42,954.64	129599.67	2009	4,89,588.40	96277.56
1994	4,46,779.90	125312.83	2010	5,11,780.20	101194.3
1995	4,55,457.90	127974.56	2011	5,07,916.80	100917.99

Year	GDP growth (1 Billion yen)	Investment growth (1 billion yen)	Capital–Output ratio
1980–1989	1,54,660.38	966275.52	6.248
1990–1999	50,352.95	1301008.18	25.838
2000–2010	33,069.60	1228984.64	37.164
1980–2010	2,38,082.93	3496268.34	14.685

Source: IMF, "World Economic Database," October 2012. Real GDP uses 2005 as the base year for constant prices. Real investment is calculated by taking the investment rate and multiplying it by constant-price GDP.

Table A.5 Equity Index and Property Price Gain and Growth in US Household Debt

Year	Composite 10CSXR-SA	Year	Household debt (US$100 billion)	Year	Total market capitalization of listed companies (US$100 billion)
1987	63.1	1990	2,606.30	1988	2,790.00
1988	70.76	1991	2,774.32	1989	3,510.00
1989	78.33	1992	2,941.75	1990	3,060.00
1990	82.65	1993	3,100.67	1991	4,090.00
1991	78.87	1994	3,277.92	1992	4,490.00
1992	78.07	1995	3,445.38	1993	5,136.20
1993	76.89	1996	3,668.42	1994	5,067.02
1994	76.06	1997	3,902.57	1995	6,857.62
1995	77.2	1998	4,259.02	1996	8,484.43
1996	76.99	1999	4,760.00	1997	11,308.78
1997	78.57	2000	5,510.00	1998	13,451.35
1998	83.26	2001	5,930.00	1999	16,635.11
1999	90.71	2002	6,660.00	2000	15,104.04
2000	100.75	2003	8,065.50	2001	13,854.62
2001	115.43	2004	9,041.60	2002	11,098.10
2002	124.83	2005	10,002.20	2003	14,266.27
2003	143.86	2006	11,313.30	2004	16,323.73
2004	164.01	2007	12,371.60	2005	16,970.87
2005	194.6	2008	12,669.90	2006	19,425.86
2006	223.87	2009	12,166.10	2007	19,947.28
2007	222.73	2010	11,713.20	2008	11,737.65
2008	197.4	2011	11,536.80	2009	15,077.29
2009	159.13			2010	17,138.98
2010	159.18				
2011	155.75				
2012	149.39				

Source: Figures for household debt prior to 1999 used Federal Housing Finance Agency data. Available at: http://www.fhfa.gov/Default.aspx?Page=70. Data for household debt after 1999 used US Federal Reserve data. Available at: http://www.federalreserve.gov/econresdata/default.htm. This data is total household debt.

Table A.6 Annual US Capital Outflows and Trade Surplus: 1978–2011

Year	Current account deficit (US$100 billion)	Current account surplus as share of GDP (%)	Foreign direct investment net outflows (US$100 billion)	Foreign direct investment net outflows as a share of GDP (%)	GDP (US$100 billion)
1978	15.75	–0.69	14.72	0.65	2276.0
1979	0.16	–0.01	25.37	1	2543.5
1980	–2.13	0.08	19.23	0.69	2767.5
1981	–4.81	0.15	9.62	0.31	3103.8
1982	11.61	–0.36	–0.98	–0.03	3227.7
1983	44.22	–1.26	7.74	0.22	3506.9
1984	99.01	–2.54	12.35	0.32	3900.4
1985	124.46	–2.97	14.06	0.34	4184.8
1986	147.17	–3.33	24.00	0.54	4425.0
1987	160.65	–3.42	35.03	0.75	4698.9
1988	121.26	–2.4	22.53	0.45	5061.9
1989	99.51	–1.83	43.45	0.8	5439.7
1990	78.95	–1.37	37.20	0.65	5750.8
1991	–2.85	0.05	37.90	0.64	5930.7
1992	51.61	–0.82	48.27	0.77	6261.8
1993	84.78	–1.29	83.95	1.28	6582.9
1994	121.64	–1.74	80.18	1.15	6993.3
1995	113.56	–1.55	98.78	1.35	7338.4
1996	124.73	–1.61	91.88	1.19	7751.1
1997	140.73	–1.7	104.82	1.27	8256.5
1998	215.04	–2.46	142.64	1.63	8741.0
1999	301.65	–3.24	224.93	2.42	9301.0
2000	416.34	–4.21	159.21	1.61	9898.8
2001	396.60	–3.88	142.35	1.39	10233.9
2002	457.25	–4.32	154.46	1.46	10590.2
2003	519.09	–4.68	149.56	1.35	11089.3
2004	628.52	–5.33	316.22	2.68	11797.8
2005	745.78	–5.94	36.24	0.29	12564.3
2006	800.62	–6.01	244.92	1.84	13314.5
2007	710.30	–5.09	414.04	2.97	13961.8
2008	677.14	–4.76	329.08	2.31	14219.3
2009	376.55	–2.72	303.61	2.19	13863.6
2010	470.90	–3.26	351.35	2.43	14447.1
2011	473.44	–3.14	406.24	2.69	15094.0

Source: World Bank data. Available at: http://data.worldbank.org.cn/indicator.

Table A.7 The increase in Scale of the US Financial Industry: 1960–2011

Year	Broad money supply M2 (US$100 billion)	Finance industry's financial assets (US$100 billion)	Total market value of the global OTC derivatives (US$100 billion)	Year	Broad money supply M2 (US$100 billion)	Finance industry's financial assets (US$100 billion)	Total market value of the global OTC derivatives (US$100 billion)
1960	353.0	682.8		1986	3677.8	10056.9	
1961	384.5	746.0		1987	3927.5	11008.3	
1962	420.3	800.0		1988	4136.4	12004.4	
1963	458.3	873.2		1989	4247.2	13258.8	
1964	497.8	954.4		1990	4310.9	13804.4	
1965	521.3	1042.3		1991	4304.3	14973.6	
1966	574.9	1101.6		1992	4330.0	16098.5	
1967	625.3	1212.4		1993	4347.5	17759.3	
1968	631.3	1333.9		1994	4646.1	19025.1	
1969	702.0	1407.6		1995	5011.6	21403.8	
1970	799.9	1526.6		1996	5412.7	23758.6	
1971	908.6	1720.7		1997	5932.4	27026.2	
1972	1001.1	1969.3		1998	6496.5	30604.9	3231.5
1973	1079.7	2160.9		1999	7023.4	34762.0	2813.4
1974	1189.6	2295.5		2000	7547.5	36508.3	3183.1
1975	1311.0	2553.7		2001	7879.3	38214.1	3788.2
1976	1468.8	2854.2		2002	8231.2	38931.0	6359.8
1977	1634.3	3182.7		2003	8702.1	43706.5	6987.2
1978	1794.4	3652.0		2004	9411.7	47824.3	9405.3
1979	1986.0	4134.3		2005	10261.1	51973.9	9799.7
1980	2225.6	4662.1		2006	11466.2	57995.0	9790.8
1981	2448.9	5176.4		2007	12405.4	63739.4	15802.5
1982	2651.4	5767.8		2008	12316.6	62341.9	35280.7
1983	2983.8	6514.9		2009	12068.3	64055.5	21541.6
1984	3231.2	7388.6		2010	12987.6	64653.8	21296.1
1985	3534.1	8768.4		2011		66067.0	27277.7

Source: World Bank, Bank for International Settlements, US Bureau of Economic Analysis (BEA).

Table A.8 US Finance Industry and Corporate Profits: 1940–2011

Year	Total corporate profits (US$100 billion)	Finance industry profits (US$100 billion)	Finance profits as share of total corporate profits (%)
1940	9.4	1.1	11.70%
1941	14.9	1.1	7.38%
1942	20.1	1.2	5.97%
1943	24.4	1.3	5.33%
1944	24.4	1.6	6.56%
1945	19.9	1.6	8.04%
1946	17.2	2.1	12.21%
1947	22.5	1.7	7.56%
1985	1177.6	179.2	15.22%
1986	1098.6	220.9	20.11%
1987	1279.4	239.7	18.74%
1998	2838.6	663.6	23.38%
1999	2939.0	805.1	27.39%
2000	2694.4	824.3	30.59%
2010	5203.5	1534.9	29.50%
2011	5552.3	1524	27.45%

Note: The finance industry includes finance and insurance companies, banks and other holding companies.

Source: US Bureau of Economic Analysis (BEA). Available at: http://www.bea.gov/.

Table A.9 US Dollar Issuance and Deficit Value: 1980–2011

Year	Fiscal deficit (US$100 billion)	Total government debt (US$100 billion)	Government debt as share of GDP (%)	Broad money supply M2 (US$100 billion)	Broad money supply growth rate (%)
1980	73.83	1,178.73	42.277	1986.01	10.67933
1981	78.97	1,294.82	41.41	2225.61	12.06443
1982	127.98	1,504.58	46.249	2448.89	10.03221
1983	207.80	1,740.79	49.25	2651.44	8.271258
1984	185.37	2,000.69	50.896	2983.76	12.53332
1985	212.31	2,351.23	55.75	3231.20	8.293099
1986	221.23	2,640.30	59.199	3534.14	9.375453
1987	149.73	2,886.84	60.951	3677.79	4.06452
1988	155.18	3,159.26	61.941	3927.55	6.79098
1989	152.64	3,410.39	62.209	4136.39	5.317363
1990	221.04	3,706.53	63.9	4247.16	2.677963
1991	269.24	4,097.63	68.384	4310.89	1.500508
1992	290.32	4,486.29	70.736	4304.29	–0.15317
1993	255.05	4,828.30	72.417	4329.96	0.596429
1994	203.19	5,071.77	71.583	4347.48	0.404669
1995	163.95	5,272.90	71.115	4646.12	6.869219
1996	107.43	5,510.36	70.299	5011.56	7.865489
1997	21.88	5,648.94	67.795	5412.66	8.003498
1998	–69.27	5,678.17	64.573	5932.38	9.601898
1999	–125.61	5,690.94	60.843	6496.46	9.508533
2000	–236.24	5,456.86	54.835	7023.35	8.110464
2001	–128.24	5,631.38	54.747	7547.48	7.462693
2002	157.76	6,078.71	57.118	7879.30	4.396333
2003	377.59	6,732.68	60.425	8231.21	4.466293
2004	412.73	8,092.13	68.269	8702.09	5.720639
2005	318.35	8,566.60	67.865	9411.70	8.154553
2006	248.18	8,912.57	66.625	10261.12	9.025161
2007	160.72	9,421.75	67.161	11466.24	11.74446
2008	454.82	10,881.09	76.137	12405.41	8.190798
2009	1,412.70	12,528.13	89.655	12316.62	–0.71575
2010	1,293.50	14,298.36	98.617	12068.31	–2.01607
2011	1,295.60	15,517.37	102.93	12987.62	7.617591

Source: Congressional Budget Office, IMF, World Bank.

Table A.10 Fogel's Estimates for GDP and Annual Growth of Major Countries in 2000 and 2040

	2000				2040				2000–2040 average growth rate (%)		
Country/regional grouping	**Population (100 million)**	**Ratio (%)**	**GDP (US$ trillion PPP)**	**Ratio (%)**	**Population (100 million)**	**Ratio (%)**	**GDP (US$ trillion PPP)**	**Ratio (%)**	**Population**	**GDP**	**Per capita GDP**
US	2.82	5	9.601	22	3.92	5	41.944	14	0.8	3.8	2.8
EU (15 nations)	3.78	6	9.264	21	3.76	4	15.04	5	0.0	1.2	1.2
India	10.03	16	2.375	5	15.22	17	36.528	12	1.0	7.1	6.0
China	13.69	22	4.951	11	14.55	17	123.675	40	0.2	8.4	8.0
Japan	1.27	2	3.456	8	1.08	1	5.292	2	–0.4	1.1	1.5
South Asia (six nations/regions)	3.81	6	2.552	6	5.16	6	35.604	12	0.8	6.8	6.0
Subtotal	35.4	58	32.119	73	43.69	50	258.083	85	0.5	5.3	4.8
Other countries/regions	25.46	42	12.307	28	43.32	50	49.774	16	1.3	3.6	2.2
Global total	60.86	99	44.506	101	87.01	100	307.857	101	0.9	5.0	4.0

Note: Due to rounding, some of the calculations will not equal 100%.

Source: Robert Fogel, "Capitalism and Democracy in 2040: Forecasts and Speculations," NBER Working Paper, No. 13184, 2007.

References

Adolf A. Berle and Gardiner C. Means, "Xiandaigongsi yu Siyoucaichan [The Modern Corporation and Private Property]," Trans. Gan Huaming, The Commercial Press, 2005, Transaction Publishers, 1991.

Erik G. Furubotn and Rudolf Richter, "Xinzhidu Jingjixue: Yige Jiaoyi Feiyong Fenxi Fanshi [Institutions and Economic Theory: The Contribution of the New Institutional Economics]," Trans. Jiang Jianqiang and Luo Changyuan, SJPC, Shanghai People's Press, 2006.

Ezra Vogel, "Riben Minglie Diyi: Dui Meiguo de Jiaoxun [Japan as Number One: Lessons for America]," Trans. Gu Ying, World Affairs Press, 1980.

Yasukichi Yasuba and Inoki Takenori (ed.), "Riben Jingjishi: Di 8 Juan [Economic History of Japan; Volume 8]," Trans. Lian Xiang, Joint Publishing, 1997; Kobayashi Yoshio, "Zhanhou Riben Jingjishi [Post-War Economic History of Japan]," Trans. Sun Hanchao and Ma Junlei, The Commercial Press, 1985.

Angus Maddison, "Shijie Jingji Qiannianshi [The World Economy: A Millennial Perspective by Angus Maddison]," Trans. Wu Xiaoying, Peking University Press, OECD, 2003.

Angus Maddison, "Zhongguo Jingji de Changqi Biaoxian — Gongyuan 960-2030 nian [Chinese Economic Performance in the Long Run]," Trans. Wu Xiaoying, Shanghai People's Press, 2008.

Barry Eichengreen, Donghyun Park and Kwanho Shin, "Kuaisu Zengzhang de Jingjiti Heshi Jiansu: Guoji Zhengju Jiqi DuiZhongguo de Qishi [When Fast Growing Economies Slow Down: International Evidence and Implications for China]," Comparative Studies, China CITIC Press 2012, Vol. 2.

Paul A. Baran and Paul M. Sweezy, "Longduan Ziben [Monopoly Capital: An Essay on the American Economic and Social Order]," Trans. Nankai University Political Economics Dept., The Commercial Press, 1977.

Paul Kennedy, "Daguo de Xingshuai: 1500–2000 nian de Jingji Bianqian yu Junshi Chongtu [The Rise and Fall of the Great Powers: Economic Change & Military Conflict from 1500 to 2000]," China International Culture Press, 2006.

Kenichi Ohmae, "M-Xing Shehui: Zhongchan jieji Xiaoshi de Weiji yu Shangji [M-form Society: The Crisis and Opportunity of the Disappearing Middle Class]," Trans. Liu Jinxiu and Jiang Yuzhen, CITIC Publishing House, 2010.

David Coates, "Ziben Zhuiyimoshi [Models of Capitalism: Growth and Stagnation in the Modern Era]," Trans. Geng Xiulin and Zong Zhaochang, Jiangsu People's Publishing, 2001.

Daniel Yergin, "Nengyuan Chongsu Shijie [The Quest: Energy, Security, and the Remaking of the Modern World]," Trans. Zhu Yuben, Petroleum Industry Publishing House, 2012.

Gu Chaoming, "Dashuaitui — Ruhe zai Jinrong Weijizhong Xincun he Fazhan [How to Survive the Financial Crisis and Develop]," Trans. Yu Haixiang, Orient Press, 2008.

Friedrich August Hayek, "Wujia yu Shengchan [Prices and Production]," Shanghai People's Press, 1958.

Jeremy Rifkin, "Disanci Gongye Geming — Xinjingji Moshi Ruhe Gaibian Shijie," Trans. Zhang Tiwei and Sun Yuning, CITIC Press Group, 2012.

Lester R. Brown, "Shengtai Jingji [Eco-Economy]," Trans. Lin Zixin and Ji Shouzhi, The Eastern Publishing Company, 2002.

Harrod Roy, "Dongtai Jingjixue [Towards a Dynamic Economics]," Trans. Huang Fanzhang, The Commercial Press, 1981.

Michael Useem, "Touzi Shang Zibenzhuyi: Yige Dianfu Jingli Zhiwei de Shidai [Investor Capitalism]," Trans. Fan Zhigang, Hainan Press, 1999.

Mancur Olson, "Guojia de Xingshuai — Jingji Zengchang, Zhizhang he Shehui Jianghua [The Rise and Decline of Nations: Economic Growth, Stagflation, and Social Rigidities]," Trans. Li Zenggang, Shanghai People's Press, 2007.

Milton Friedman and Rose Friedman, "Ziyou Xuanze [Free to Choose: A Personal Statement]," Trans. Zhang Qi, China Machine Press, 2008.

Thomas L. Friedman, "Shijie shi Pingde: 21 Shiji Jianshi [The World Is Flat: A Brief History of the Twenty-first Century]," Trans. He Fan, Hunan Science & Technology Press, 2006.

Vincent Ostrom, Elinor Ostrom and Robert Bish, "Meiguo Difang Zhengfu [Local Government in the United States]," Trans. Jing Min, Peking University Press, 2004.

Kobayashi Yoshio, "Zhanhou Riben Jingjishi [Post-War Economic History of Japan]," Trans. Sun Hanchao and Ma Junlei, The Commercial Press, 1985.

Jacques Attali, "Guojia de Pochan [State Bankruptcy]," Trans. Wu Fangyu, Beijing United Publishing, 2011.

Meredith Woo-Cumings (ed.), "Fazhanxing Guojia [The Developmental State]," Trans. Cao Haijun, Jilin Publishing Group, 2008.

John Maynard Keynes, "Jiuye, Lixi he Huobi Tonglun [The General Theory of Employment, Interest and Money]," Trans. Lu Menglong, China Social Sciences Press, 2009.

Nakamura Takafusa (ed.), "Riben Jingjishi [Economic History of Japan; Volume 7]," Trans. Hu Qilin, Hu Jing, and Lin Hua, Joint Publishing, 1997.

Karl Marx and Friedrich Engels, "Makesi Engesi Xuanji [Marx/Engels Collected Works; Volume 3]," People's Publishing House, 1995.

Karl Marx, "Zibenlun [Das Kapital]," People's Publishing House, 2004.

International Monetary Fund, World Bank, "Jinrong yu Fazhan [F&D Finance and Development]," Chinese-language edition, December 1987.

International Energy Agency, "World Energy Outlook 2007."

World Bank, "Dongya Qiji: Jingji Zengzhang yu Gonggong Zhengce [The East Asian Miracle: Economic Growth and Public Policy]," Trans. World Bank Operations Division, Ministry of Finance, China Financial & Economic Publishing house, 1995.

US Bureau of Economic Analysis (BEA). Available at: http://www.bea.gov/.

US Census Bureau, "Resident Population Data: Population Change," 2010. Available at: http://www.census.gov.

US Department of the Treasury, "Securities(d): Holdings of Long-term Securities." Available at: http://www.treasury.gov/Pages/default.aspx.

World Gold Council, "Annual time series on World Official Gold Reserves since 1845." Available at: http://www.gold.org/government_affairs/gold_reserves/.

Standard & Poor's, "S&P/CaseShiller Home Price Indices." Available at: http://www.standardandpoors.com.

Bank for International Settlements. Available at: http://www.bis.org/statistics/derstats.htm.

Federal Housing Finance Agency. Available at: http://www.fhfa.gov/Default.aspx?Page=70.

US Federal Reserve. Available at: http://www.federalreserve.gov/econresdata/default.htm.

Statistics Japan, "Historical Statistics of Japan's Gross Domestic Product Classified by Economic Activities68SNA." Available at: http://www.stat.go.jp/.

Singapore Government. Available at: http://www.gov.sg/government/web/content/govsg/classic/home.

State Council, "12th Five-year Development Plan for National Strategic Emerging Industries," National Development, 2012, No. 28. Available at: http://www.gov.cn/zwgk/2012-07/20/content_2187770.htm.

Government and Ministry Websites:

State-owned Assets Supervision and Administration Commission (SASAC). Available at: http://www.sasac.gov.cn/n1180/index.html.

Ministry of Land and Resources. Available at: http://www.mlr.gov.cn/.

Ministry of National Defense. Available at: http://www.mod.gov.cn/.

Ministry of Agriculture. Available at: http://www.moa.gov.cn/.

State Administration of Foreign Exchange (SAFE). Available at: http://www.safe.gov.cn/.

China National Tourism Administration. Available at: http://www.cnta.gov.cn/.

Ministry of Finance Budget Department. Available at: http://yss.mof.gov.cn/.

China Hong Kong SAR government. Available at: http://www.gov.hk/sc/residents/.

Shanghai Stock Exchange. Available at: http://www.sse.com.cn/.

Kunshan Statistics Bureau's, "2011 Kunshan City Economic and Social Development Report." Available at: http://www.kstj.gov.cn/.

Postscript

After I handed over the final revised draft of the text to the publisher, I let out a long, long sigh of relief. Although I have not written many books, the previous manuscripts had all been written in one go, with the drafts handed in for printing once they were done. Even when I was co-authoring with Mr Jiang Xuemo on the 12th edition of "A Textbook for Political Economics," over 200 pages was completed in just over 20 days. But this time, this small book titled "Supernormal Growth: China's Economy 1979–2049," took me half a year, altogether requiring several drafts. And when I finally handed it in, I still had a lot of regrets.

The reason it was difficult to write was because the main subject is too large, the problems too many. When I did my final read through, the sections and paragraphs on energy and ecology surprised me — how could I have devoted so much space simply to the issues of productivity?

The main topic of this book, namely supernormal growth, came to me on a whim one night in July last year (Ed.: 2012). Although the manuscript was fomented and written in just over half a year, the contents represent the results of my study and reflection in the more than 30 years since joining Fudan University's economics department in 1977. It also incorporates the observations and insights from my 18 years of working in the business world after I returned from study abroad in 1995. In some sense, this book is the real starting point for me to step out from the paradigm of modern economics and set about developing my own independent theories. Therefore, I dedicate this book to the most important person in my life — Zhaili, my wife, my best friend and my partner. Since I met her, became acquainted with her and fell in love with her, I was really able to become independent, self-confident and self-reliant. Because of her encouragement and participation, my intellectual vigor and creativity was able to shine. For me, *she is God's gift and a soundless Gospel.*

This book's main ideas and text are from the author, but the overall task of completing the research is thanks to the participation of my team — Tang Yinan, Sylvie Cai Chenfei and Gou Jinhai. Tang Yinan shouldered the responsibility of searching for much of the information, conducted the calculations and also specially designed the graphs showing the chain reaction of local government incentives; Sylvie Cai Chenfei not only looked up and verified the academic literature, assisted with data collection and calculations, but also efficiently completed a number of amendments to the typesetting; Gou Jinhai made time in his tight schedule while completing his dissertation to provide background research on the main topics of *Japan's development strategy* and environmental protection. The fruits of their fundamental work provided the support this book needed to reach the standard that it did.

From start to finish, Professors Zhang Jun, Liu Chang and Chen Ping participated in the fermentation and writing of this book. Professor Zhang Jun specially provided background documents of over 10,000 words on modern economic growth and also organized a small seminar at Fudan University's Chinese economics department in aid of this book. Professor Liu Chang participated in discussions about the overall structure of the book, as well as especially collating historical information on Chinese and US economic cycles and finding out the source of Gu Yanwu's contention about "infusing the imperial with the spirit/essence of the feudal." Chen Ping read the draft of this book from beginning to end and made many suggestions on revisions. Their views and comments ensured that this book avoided many deficiencies.

In the early stage of writing, I gave a speech on the core views of the book at a Tsinghua University political economics work forum hosted by Professor Meng Jie. At that forum, I received affirmation and suggestions that benefitted me greatly from Mr Huang Zhongzhi, Professor Cui Zhiyuan and Professor Zhu Tianbiao as well as others.

Once I had written a draft, I asked many colleagues and friends in the academic community to read through the manuscript and offer their opinions for revisions and many did provide valuable ideas for amendments. They were: Chen Jiajia, Fan Yongjin, Feng Jiansong and Hong Yinxing, and Liu Ji, Liu Lili, Pan Yi, Pan Yingli, Qin Shaode, Sheng Liantao, Wang Shao Guang, Wei Lin, Xiao Geng, Yin Tongyue, Zhang Weiwei, Zhang Wuchang, Zhao Haiying, Deng Yongnian and Zhou Lin. I extend my sincere thanks to all of you.

Before the manuscript was sent off for printing, Beijing University's National School of Development arranged a small seminar for me. Professors Justin Lin Yifu, Zhang Shuguang and Tao Yang made many pertinent and profound comments from many different angles that gave me great encouragement and clarified the path for further research ideas.

Finally and most crucially is Mr Chen Xin, chief executive officer of Shanghai Century Publishing Group. Without his inspiration and encouragement, the writing of this book would not have so quickly entered the planning stage. Without his resolve and prodding, this book would not have been finished in time. Without his guidance and editing, this book would not have achieved the standard that it has! Thank you, from the bottom of my heart.

China's rapid economic development is destined to become a major event in world economic history. In practice, the socialist market economic system with Chinese characteristics will inevitably become a major innovation in the history of human institutions. In the book, I am able to reveal the innovation of this Chinese-style system. Apart from the years of study and practice, even more important to my inspiration was the businessmen and government officials at every level working on the front lines. In my roughly 18-year career in corporate management and investment, from the deserts of Xinjiang to the grassy plains of Inner Mongolia, from the coasts of Jiangsu and Zhejiang to the central plains, I was fortunate enough to meet hundreds of businessmen and government officials whom I exchanged ideas with and learned from, allowing me to see a new world that I could not have previously imagined. They are just like ordinary people with their own ideas, aspirations, personalities and also, of course, weaknesses. But most of them, with their own supernormal enthusiasm and excess workloads have driven China's progress! They are also the angels of the new era. Many of the views of this book come from observing them in action and learning from them over countless dialogues and discussions. Friends, you all know that I cannot name you all here. I hope that one day you will be able to share your life experiences and stories with everyone. Please allow me to salute you all here in the name of reform! I salute all those who earnestly care for China's development and all those who have contributed to the realization of "Chinese dream"!

Jeffrey Shi Zhengfu
April 24, 2013
Pudong, Shanghai

Index